Job Satisfaction of Bank Employees After a Merger and Acquisition

by

DR. MICHAEL C. MADU

Ordering Information:

For orders and inquiries, please contact:
1-888-404-1388
www.goldtouchpress.com
book.orders@goldtouchpress.com

Printed in the United States of America

TABLE OF CONTENTS

Dedication ix
Acknowledgments xi
Abstract xiii

Chapter 1: Foundation of the Study 1
Background of the Problem 1
Problem Statement 2
Purpose Statement 3
Nature of the Study 3
Research Question 4
Hypotheses 4
    Survey Questions 5
Theoretical Framework 5
Definition of Terms 6
Assumptions, Limitations, and Delimitations 7
    Assumptions 7
    Limitations 8
    Delimitations 8
Significance of the Study 8
    Contribution to Business Practice 8
    Implications for Social Change 9
A Review of the Professional and Academic Literature 10
    History of Bank M&A 33
    M&As as a Strategy 35
    Failed Mergers: Contributing Factors 43
    Employee Satisfaction or Dissatisfaction 49
Transition and Summary 51

Chapter 2:   The Project 52
  Purpose Statement 52
  Role of the Researcher 53
  Participants...53
  Research Method and Design...55
    Method 55
    Research Design...56
  Population and Sampling 57
  Ethical Research...58
  Data Collection 58
    Instruments 58
    Data Collection Technique..59
    Data Organization Techniques..60
  Data Analysis Technique..60
  Reliability and Validity 62
    Reliability...62
    Validity...63
  Transition and Summary..64

Chapter 3:   Application to Professional Practice and
             Implications for Change 66
  Overview of Study 66
  Presentation of the Findings..68
    Preliminary Analysis 68
    Primary Analysis 87
  Summary...89
  Applications to Professional Practice..92
  Implications for Social Change 93
  Recommendations for Action...94
  Recommendations for Further Study 95
  Reflections 95
  Summary and Study Conclusions 96

References 99

Appendix A: Questionnaire 119

Appendix B: Email Invitation to Participants 127

Appendix C: The Follow-up Invitation E-mail 129

Appendix D: Permission to use the JDI and AJIG Scales 131

Appendix E: Letter to the Bank 133

Appendix F: SurveyMonkey® Confidentiality
and Security Policy 135

Appendix G: Informed Consent Form 137

Appendix H: AJDI/AJIG Scoring Model......................139

Appendix I: JDI Office – Terms of Use 141

Appendix J: SurveyMonkey® Terms of Use 145

LIST OF TABLES

Table 1:   Summary of Various Sources of the Literature 10

Table 2:   Frequencies and Percentages for Categorical
           Independent Variables..69

Table 3:   Frequencies and Percentages for Age, Race,
           Education Level, Job Level, and Years with
           Organization by Gender..71

Table 4:   Frequencies and Percentages for Gender, Race,
           Education Level, Job Level, and Years with
           Organization by Age 75

Table 5:   Frequencies and Percentages for Gender, Age,
           Education Level, Job Level, and Years with
           Organization by Race...77

Table 6:   Frequencies and Percentages for Gender, Age,
           Race, Job Level, and Years with Organization by
           Education Level 81

Table 7:   Frequencies and Percentages for Gender,
           Age, Race, Education Level, and Years with
           Organization by Job Level 83

Table 8:   Frequencies and Percentages for Gender, Age,
           Race, Education Level, and Job Level by Years
           with Organization 85

Table 9:   Means and Standard Deviations for JIG Sum Score......87

Table 10: One-Way ANOVAs for JIG Sum Score by
          Gender, Age, Race, Education Level, Job Level,
          and Years with Organization...88

Table 11: Similarities and Differences Between Current
          Study and Baker (2009)...91

Dedication

My dedication goes to my three very special children, Chiamaka (daughter), Chidera (daughter), and Chinonso (son), whom I intensely love, and of course my dear wife, Queen Nkiruka "Eggyolk" Madu, for her love and understanding. To my father, Ogbuehi Charles Ejiribeoffor Madu, for instilling self confidence in me at an early age; and always reminded me that I can reach the moon if I choose to and work hard at it. Finally, to my mother, Janet Madu: For her unconditional love.

Acknowledgments

I wish to thank Dr. Karin Mae, Chairperson of my Doctoral Study Research Committee, for her leadership, feedback and encouragement. And thanks to The Job Descriptive Index (JDI) Research Group, Department of Psychology, Bowling Green State University, Bowling Green, Ohio, United States, for giving me the permission to use the Abridged Job in General (AJIG) scale in this research.

My profound thanks to individuals too many to mention here; such as my brothers, sisters, uncles, in-laws, and cousins who have been sources of inspiration and support.

Abstract

Guided by social identity theory, the purpose of this quantitative descriptive study was to examine potential factors affecting bank employees' job satisfaction and strategies to help bank leaders forestall the exit of top-performing bank employees from the banks after the M&A. Bank leadership needs the support of employees to achieve the strategic goals for mergers and acquisitions (M&A). The exit of unhappy employees from the banks after the M&A limits the leaders' ability to achieve the goals. A review of literature showed that employees may leave banks employment after an M&A from job dissatisfaction. Adequate research about the factors affecting job satisfaction of bank employees after an M&A does not exist. The effects of demographic factors of race, gender, job tenure, job level, age, and level of education on job satisfaction of bank employees post merger were examined. Using online survey, data were collected from 217 employees experiencing an M&A between January 2006 and December 2009 with Sunshine Bank (pseudonym), in Bucks, Delaware, Montgomery, and Philadelphia counties of Pennsylvania. I analyzed the respondents' data via analysis of variance at the .05 significance level. The effects of age, level of education, job position, or job tenure of employees on post merger job satisfaction levels were significant at the .05 levels. Findings from this study may create beneficial social change as future bank administrators implement social identity theory-based strategies validated by this research. The administrators will be better positioned to meet the demands of the stakeholders regarding employment, higher rate of return and sustainability of business.

CHAPTER 1

Foundation of the Study

Mergers and acquisitions (M&A) are among the solutions banks' leaders use as the leaders attempt to survive, lead, or dominate the industry (Chu, 2010). Leaders of banks could use M&A as a growth strategy in the face of rising competition. M&A are means to reduce or eliminate competition, reach a broader market, and use any technological advantage, product, service efficiency, or synergy that may exist between the merging companies (Ashton, 2012).

M&A administrators often fail to achieve the expected benefits that necessitated the M&A in the first place (Ben Slama, Fedhila, & Saidane, 2012; Garbuio, Horn, & Lovallo, 2010). One reason could be employees' states of mind, as unhappy employees usually underperform (Crawford, Lepine, & Rich, 2010; Kumar, Pak, & Rose, 2009). Baker (2009) found that the job satisfaction of employees is a critical factor to determine whether a merger will be successful. Employee job satisfaction is a determinant of organizational performance (Kumar et al., 2011). Given the evidence in literature on how the job satisfaction of bank employees affects the success or failure of an M&A, I chose to examine the factors affecting job satisfaction of bank employees post M&A in the current study. The goal was to make any discoveries available to future bank leaders, and perhaps provide new information that may help the bank executives in managing and leading future banks' M&A.

BACKGROUND OF THE PROBLEM

Through M&A, leaders of banks seek to reach wider markets, eliminate competition, and maximize opportunities with the expectation to achieve higher returns for the stakeholders (Chu,

2010). Bank leaders use M&A as a strategy to raise additional capital to sustain the operation or generate growth (Baker, 2009). Bank leaders do not always achieve the expected increase in profit and market share after an M&A (Beccalli & Frantz, 2009). Because of the potential failures, I examined reasons merger goals are not attained to help create strategies which will lead to successful future M&A. Adjei-Benin and Sanda (2011) found that companies undergoing M&A tend to ignore the human emotions involved. Unmanaged human emotions can generate low morale and lead to a decline in productivity (Baker, 2009). If bank leaders learned to identify key drivers necessary to motivate employees and create job satisfaction, the leaders could foster an environment that promotes top performance, retention of important employees, and achievement of the goals of the M&A.

PROBLEM STATEMENT

The exit of top performers, including leaders from banks, is a problem leaders of banks experience after M&A (Georgiades & Georgiades, 2014; Krug, 2009). The goal of M&A is to make the merged banks strategically stronger, but the exit of valuable employees from the merged banks makes the realization of this goal difficult (Konstantopoulos, Sakas, & Triantafyllopoulos, 2009; Krug, 2009). According to Krug (2009), 70% of top executives leave within years of the M&A. Good employees leave the merged banks because of dissatisfaction and anxiety over the merger (Baker, 2009; Georgiades & Georgiades, 2014; Konstantopoulos et al., 2009; Krug, 2009). The general business-related problem is the inability of a bank's leaders to achieve the stated goals of the merger. The specific business-related problem is that some banks' managers lack strategies for stopping the exit of top-performing employees, including leaders from the banks after M&A.

PURPOSE STATEMENT

The purpose of this quantitative research study was to examine factors that influence the exit of top-performing employees, including leaders from the banks after the M&A from the perspectives of job tenure, job title, race, age, gender, or level of education of the bank employees. Using a quantitative descriptive design, I examined the effects of the stated factors on satisfaction levels post merger. Job tenure, job title, race, age, gender, and level of education were the independent variables and job satisfaction was the dependent variable.

The specific population group studied was bank employees who experienced M&A between 2006 and 2009. I obtained the sample of participants from Sunshine Bank (pseudonym). I contacted the participants through e-mails (see Appendix B), requesting them to complete the survey posted on SurveyMonkey® (see Appendix A). I did not send reminders (see Appendix C) to participants because I received the expected number of participants and responses within 7 days as planned. Sunshine Bank's employees work in several different states in the United States. For the research to be more manageable in scope, I conducted the study on employees in Bucks, Delaware, Montgomery, and Philadelphia counties of Pennsylvania.

Bank executives could use the information obtained from the research to manage future mergers in manners that will minimize or eliminate employee anxieties, turnover, and job losses. If more mergers are effectively managed and successful, more employees could be retained. The employed individuals could support their families, and perhaps contribute to building better communities.

NATURE OF THE STUDY

I used a quantitative method to conduct the research. In the research, I examined the level of job satisfaction among bank employees who experienced M&A, between 2006 and 2009. I examined the data to determine the extent each independent variable affected the level of job satisfaction. I further examined the collected data using statistical analysis of variance (ANOVA) at significance level of .05. Quantitative research method is suitable for explaining phenomena, by collecting numerical data and analyzing the data through a statistically based method (Muijs, 2004). After I collected the data, I proceeded with the ANOVA for the analysis. Qualitative data are not usually numerical (Muijs, 2004). Qualitative method focuses on the quality and texture of participants' experience (Willig, 2013). The quantitative method was most appropriate because I required numerical data to analyze and address the principal research question.

RESEARCH QUESTION

What strategies could help bank leaders to forestall the exit of top-performing bank employees, including leaders from the banks after the M&A? I examined the job satisfaction of bank employees after the M&A from the perspectives of job tenure, job level, race, age, gender, and level of education to determine if the demographic factors had any effect on the job satisfaction levels of the bank employees who experienced M&A, and whether the level of job satisfaction affected the employees' decision to stay or leave the bank after the M&A. The information was important to help examine if job satisfaction has any effect on the job performance of employees (Baker, 2009). Job satisfaction could affect retention. Satisfied employees are likely to stay with the bank after the merger, and unhappy employees could leave (Krug, 2009).

HYPOTHESES

$H1_0$: There is no effect of job tenure on job satisfaction for bank employees who have experienced M&A.

$H1_a$: There is an effect of job tenure on job satisfaction for bank employees who have experienced M&A.

$H2_0$: There is no effect of race on job satisfaction for bank employees who have experienced M&A.

$H2_a$: There is an effect of race on job satisfaction for bank employees who have experienced M&A.

$H3_0$: There is no effect of age on job satisfaction for bank employees who have experienced M&A.

$H3_a$: There is an effect of age on job satisfaction for bank employees who have experienced M&A.

$H4_0$: There is no effect of gender on job satisfaction for bank employees who have experienced M&A.

$H4_a$: There is an effect of gender on job satisfaction for bank employees who have experienced M&A.

$H5_0$: There is no effect of level of education on job satisfaction for bank employees who have experienced M&A.

$H5_a$: There is an effect of level of education on job satisfaction for bank employees who have experienced M&A.

$H6_0$: There is no effect of job level or position on job satisfaction for bank employees who have experienced M&A.

$H6_a$: There is an effect of job level or position on job satisfaction for bank employees who have experienced M&A on job satisfaction.

Survey Questions

See appendix A.

THEORETICAL FRAMEWORK

The current research was examined through the theoretical framework of social identity theory (SIT). SIT refers to the bond and group identification individuals exhibit from belonging to the same group or sharing a common cause (Schmidts & Shepherd, 2013). SIT was developed by Tajfel, a British social psychologist, in conjunction with his student, Turner, in 1979 (Haslam, Reynolds, & Reicher, 2012). This group identification can be powerful and could be a source of social or political change (Schmidts & Shepherd, 2013). Individuals identify with their groups and the group identity could be a source of pride, forum for social demand and change, action, and solidarity (Schmidts & Shepherd, 2013). Individuals can also develop social identity as a result of working together. The exit of valuable bank employees after an M&A disrupts the social identity formed by the employees from working together (Baker, 2009). The disruption of the social identity could become a de-motivator and create job dissatisfaction. This could contribute to the departure of more employees after the M&A. The employees may feel a lowered sense of self-worth and decreased values of their jobs (Kitamura, Sakata, & Takagishi, 2012).

Organization leaders positively can influence the attitudes of employees (Nadiri & Tanova, 2010). Nadiri and Tanova (2010) found that high performance is achieved, and organizational goals met when employee morale is high. Organizations could achieve this by adhering to the concept of the equity theory. Adams developed the equity theory in 1963 that individuals are motivated relative to the compensation in the same line of work and position (Okoro, 2010). The perception of fairness is an important factor in the management and motivation of employees (Okoro, 2010; Tudor, 2011). Banks' leaders should be conscious of the equity theory while implementing any M&A.

DEFINITION OF TERMS

Abridged job descriptive index: Survey instrument used in measuring job satisfaction level (Abrahamson & Bormann, 2014).

Age: The number of years describing how old an individual is (De Lange, Dikkers, Jansen, & Kooij, 2010).

Company acquisition: When one company buys the entire assets or specific assets of another company (Brock, Calipha, & Tarba, 2010; Georgiades & Georgiades, 2014).

Equity theory: Belief that an equal amount and the same level of work should be rewarded equally (Okoro, 2010).

Gender: The state of being male or female (Agier & Szafarz, 2013).

Job descriptive index: Survey instrument used in measuring job satisfaction level (Abrahamson & Bormann, 2014).

Job satisfaction: The emotional fulfillment derived by individuals from their jobs (Cleare, 2013).

Merger and acquisition: These two words are interchangeable (Adebisi & Oghojafor, 2012).

Stochastic frontier analysis: Efficient economic method for measuring economic models (Dollery, Villano, & Wijeweera, 2010).

Too-big-to-fail: The belief that the size of a bank or company is such that the failure of the bank or company will have a catastrophic effect on the financial system or economy (Brewer & Jagtiani, 2011).

ASSUMPTIONS, LIMITATIONS, AND DELIMITATIONS

Assumptions

An assumption was that the respondents put personal biases aside and responded objectively and truthfully to the survey. No evidence exists that the participants put aside personal biases and responded objectively and truthfully. The participants could have personal biases that interfered with the result of the survey. I am unable to discern from the completed surveys whether personal biases influenced the responses or not.

An assumption was that the respondents were interested in the accuracy of the results. I found no evidence to confirm or fail to confirm that the respondents were interested in the accuracy of the results. I could not determine from the completed surveys if the respondents were truthful or not.

The sample studied may not be a good representation of the population of bank employees. Purposeful sampling was used to select the participants. This approach is not completely random and requires the results of this study to be cautiously interpreted (Springer, 2010).

An assumption was that participants understood the variables used in this study similarly. The effect of each demographic variable and how the employee perceives it in different geographic locations could be different. I was not able to discern from the completed surveys the extent, if any, that geographic location influenced or failed to influence the responses. This bias, if true, could limit the external validity of this study.

Limitations

The satisfaction of employees before the M&A was not known so no comparison could be made. The survey did not account for items, such as goal emphasis, role stress, work ethic, autonomy, and job challenge, which have been identified as important factors of job satisfaction (Chen, Lien, & Lin, 2011). I did not examine the effect of other stressors that could have affected the level of satisfaction.

The experiences of the employees were from one major bank in Pennsylvania and may not reflect the experiences of employees from banks in other states. Personal bias based on the employees' experiences probably influenced responses and interfered with the objectivity of the participants. The participants were asked to set their personal biases aside, but no evidence exists that the participants complied or not.

Delimitations

The population studied was from one bank with employees in Bucks, Delaware, Montgomery, and Philadelphia counties of Pennsylvania. The experience or response of the bank's employees in other areas of Pennsylvania and other states may be different. In addition, the experiences of bank employees from other banks who experienced M&A could be different.

SIGNIFICANCE OF THE STUDY

Contribution to Business Practice

The results of this study add to the existing literature and provide additional information to banks and other business leaders in understanding the effects of factors such as job tenure, job title, race, age, gender, or level of education on job satisfaction as a strategy to help stop the exit of top-performing employees, including leaders from banks after an M&A. The information could help to reduce or eliminate the turnover seen in banks, especially after the M&A (Krug, 2009). Leaders of banks could use the information to improve on how they manage the exit of valuable employees after an M&A.

Brakman, Garretsen, Marrewijk, and Witteloostuijn (2013) identified M&A as strategic tool for global businesses that seek growth, diversification, or profitability. Mylonakis (2006) found that about 25% of the M&A that occur in the United States are in the banking sector. However, M&A administrators often fail to achieve the intended goals of an M&A such as growth in profits and market share. The morale and behavior of employees are fundamental factors to achieving the intended goals of an M&A (Austin & Benton, 2010). If employees have high job satisfaction and positive morale, performance will be high, thereby putting the organization in a better position for success (Austin & Benton, 2010). The job satisfaction of employees could contribute to increased product quality and customer satisfaction. The result of employee job satisfaction could also lead to increased employee retention (Krug, 2009).

Implications for Social Change

Executing M&A in a manner sensitive to the needs of employees will benefit the stakeholders if employees are assured that jobs are secure (Bellou, 2007). If the leaders communicate job security to the employees, that can help to boost the morale of the employees. Under this circumstance, the employees will tend to perform better and produce more for the organization (Austin & Benton, 2010). The financial returns for the shareholders may increase. The increase in the number of employees retained may help to provide the community with gainfully employed taxpayers who contribute to the economy and may perform civic duties. A successful M&A helps the organization, the community, and the shareholders to achieve the goal, and employees do not worry about job security (Bellou, 2007).

A Review of the Professional and Academic Literature

The purpose of this quantitative research study was to examine factors that influence the exits of top-performing employees, including leaders who leave banks after M&A because of job tenure, job title, race, age, gender, or level of education of the bank employees. The following was the research question for this study: What strategies could help bank leaders to forestall the exit of top-performing bank employees, including leaders from the banks after M&A? One strategy examined in this study was the job satisfaction of bank employees after M&A based on the job tenure, job title, race, age, gender, or level of education of the bank employees. This strategy was used to determine if demographic factors affected bank employees' decisions to stay or leave banks after M&A. Results showed the relationship between the satisfaction levels and demographic factors of bank employees who experienced M&A. Table 1 shows summaries of the sources included in the literature review.

Table 1

Summary of Various Sources of the Literature

Authors	Sources	Summary
Crawford, C. (2011)	*Journal of Business and Economic Research, 9, 127-133.*	Discussed bank regulations and why they became necessary.
Huang, Z., & Marquis, C. (2010)	*Academy of Management Journal, 53, 1441-1473.*	Discussed how and why M&A became growth strategies for bank leaders.

Authors	Sources	Summary
He, Y., & Zhao, R. (2014)	*Review of Quantitative Finance and Accounting, 42, 449-468.*	Talked about how bank leaders moved away from creating bank holding companies in states to moving across state lines to merge and acquire other banks.
Gaganis, C., Pasiouras, F., Tanna, S. (2011).	*Financial Markets, Institutions and Instruments, 20, 29-77*	Discussed some variables bank leaders looked at before undertaking M&A.
Boateng, A., & Uddin, M. (2011).	*International Business Review, 20, 547-556.*	Discussed cross-border M&As among different countries in the European Union (EU).
Ghobadian, A., Hitt, M. A., Kling, G., O'Regan, N., & Weitzel, U.(2014).	*British Journal of Management, 25, 116-132.*	Talked about how bank leaders moved across national borders to take advantage of perceived synergy in merging with target banks.

Authors	Sources	Summary
Beck, T., Levine, R., & Levkov, A. (2010).	*The Journal of Finance, 65, 1637-1667.*	Talked about how the era of liberalization, deregulation, and advances in technology combined to change the financial landscape, and the competition between banks and non-bank financial institutions.
Huyghebaert, N., & Luypaert, M. (2013).	*International Journal of Financial Research, 4(2), 49-67.*	Discussed how bank executives merged banks to achieve synergy and improve management of the acquired institution.

M&A as a Strategy:

Heiney, J. (2011).	*http://journals.cluteonline. com/index.php/JBER/ article/view/5638*	Talked about how new opportunities resulted in interstate banking and branching in the United States.

Authors	Sources	Summary
Phillips, G. M., & Zhdanov, A. (2013).	*Review of Financial Studies Journal, 26, 34-78.*	Discussed why several bank leaders resort to M&As as growth strategies
Assaf, A. G., Barros, C., & Ibiwoye, A. (2012).	*The Service Industries Journal, 32, 215-230.*	Examined if M&As eliminate operating inefficiencies and reduce processing expenses for banks.
Baker, S. A. (2009).	*ProQuest Dissertations and Theses database. (UMI No. 3384714)*	Examined job satisfaction of bank employees after M&A.
Bernard, C., Fuentelsaz, L., & Gomez, J. (2010).	*Omega, 38, 283-293.*	Studied if M&As were ways to eliminate operating inefficiencies for banks.
Wheelock, D. C., & Wilson, P. W. (2012)	*Journal of Money, Credit and Banking, 44, 171-199.*	Examined if bank leaders considered to take advantage of economies of scale as they decided on undertaking M&A.

Authors	Sources	Summary
Lambkin, M. C., & Muzellec, L. (2010)	*Industrial Marketing Management, 39, 1234-1239.*	Found that in an M&A the acquirer company with the stronger brand recognition than the acquired company should consider renaming the acquired company to bear the same name as the parent company.
Hoberg, G., & Phillips, G. (2010).	*Review of Financial Studies, 23, 3773-3811.*	Examined firms that merged to take advantage of similar, but unique, product offerings.
Azan, W., & Sutter, I. H. (2010).	*Knowledge Management Research and Practice, 8, 307-321.*	Posit that successful implementation of M&As provides the opportunity for knowledge transfer between the merging firms.
Holland, W., & Salama, A. (2010).	*Learning Organization, 17, 268-283.*	Discussed relevance of knowledge transfer to M&A.

Authors	Sources	Summary
Fethi, M. D., Kumbhakar, S. C., Lozano-Vivas, A., & Shaban, M. (2011).	*Journal of Productivity Analysis, 36, 247-261.*	Examined effectiveness of the merger processes in European banks from 1998 to 2004.
Behr, A., & Heid, F. (2011).	*Journal of Empirical Finance, 18, 117-135.*	Studied profitability and cost efficiencies achieved by German banks that underwent M&A.
Evripidou, L. (2012).	*International Journal of Organizational Analysis, 20, 435-446.*	Examined pre-merger and post-merger data from two merged airline companies to determine the post-merger systematic risk and improved cost efficiencies.
Erel, I., Liao, R. C., & Weisbach, M. S. (2012).	*The Journal of Finance, 67, 1045-1082.*	Analyzed a sample of 56,978 cross-border mergers for evidence of increased valuation after merger.

Authors	Sources	Summary
Jog, V., & Zhu, P. (2012).	*Emerging Markets Finance and Trade, 48(4), 79-101.*	Studied large samples of M&A data from emerging countries. Results indicated that target firms benefit from cross-border M&A.
Bhuyan, R., Ng, S. A., & Vaziri, M. T. (2010).	*Corporate Finance: Governance, Corporate Control and Organization Journal, 7, 8-25.*	Showed that acquiring banks benefit from increased value resulting from the announcement of M&A.
Goto, N., Nogata, D., & Uchida, K. (2011).	*Journal of Economics and Business, 63(1), 46-75.*	Discussed increased value resulting from announcement of M&A.
Hamza, T. (2009).	*Journal of Management and Governance, 15, 157-186.*	Studied reported increase in value that occurs after the announcement of an M&A.
Olowe, R. (2011).	*African Journal of Economic and Management Studies, 2, 180-201.*	Results indicated that merger announcements contributed to increased valuation of banks.

Authors	Sources	Summary
Piskula, T. (2011).	*The Journal of Business and Economic Studies, 17(1), 1-15.*	Contended that on average, equity values of banks do not display positive returns upon the announcement of mergers.
Alexandridis, G., Petmezas, D., & Travlos, N. G. (2010).	*Financial Management, 39, 1671-1695.*	Discussed that acquirers in competitive takeover markets (e.g., United States, United Kingdom [UK], and Canada) benefit from the merger announcements.
Buch, C. M., Koch, C. T., & Koetter, M. (2013).	*Review of Finance, 17, 1401-1435.*	Talked about bank leaders undertaking merger ventures to gain more operating efficiency, enhanced market power, improved risk diversification, and heightened economies of scale.

Authors	Sources	Summary
Liargovas, P., & Repousis, S. (2011).	*International Journal of Economics and Finance, 3(2), 89-100.*	Contend that M&A do not create wealth.
Samet, K. (2010).	*International Journal of Economics and Finance, 2(5), 66-78.*	Found no added value resulting from M&A.
Harada, K., & Ito, T. (2011).	*Journal of the Japanese and International Economies, 25(1), 1-22.*	Found that M&A do not create incremental value for the merged banks.
Chaudhary, T., Kaushil, K. P., & Sinha, N. (2010).	*International Journal of Economics and Finance, 2(4), 190-200*	Examined pre- and post-merger efficiency of Indian Banks using ratio analysis approach and a nonparametric Wilcoxon signed-rank test to evaluate the performance of the banks.
Mehrotra, V., Spronk, J., Steenbeek, O., & van Schaik, D. (2011).	*Journal of Financial and Quantitative Analysis, 46, 1051-1088.*	Found that mergers in Japan are determined by the demands of creditors.

Authors	Sources	Summary
Mylonakis, J. (2006)	*Financial Services Management, 1, 205-214.*	Examined M&A as a strategy and the competitive advantages associated with it.
Bernile, G., Lyandres, E., & Zhdanov, A. (2011).	*Review of Finance, 16, 517-575*	Evaluated empirical evidence based on parametric and semi-parametric regression analysis and found that motivators for undertaking M&As include strong competitive interaction among firms.
Papaioannou, G. (2011).	*Journal of Financial Services Marketing, 16, 153-169.*	Found that bank leaders acquire securities firms to bolster market share.
Amine, L. S., Khan, G. M., Uddin, S. J., & Zaman, M. (2011).	*International Business Review, 53, 581-600.*	Discussed how M&A became a viable tool for internationalization of banks.
Mili, M., & Sahut, J. (2011).	*Economic Modelling, 28, 138-146.*	Discussed role of synergy in bank mergers.

Authors	Sources	Summary
García-Suaza, A. F., & Gómez-González, J. E. (2010).	*Economic Systems, 34, 437-449.*	Found that solvency, size of the firm, and efficiency levels are key determinants of acquisition opportunity.
Hankir, Y., Rauch, C., & Umber, M. P. (2011).	*Journal of Banking and Finance, 35, 2341-2354.*	Contend that M&A provide opportunities for global diversification.
Li, S., Qiu, J., & Wan, C. (2011).	*Journal of International Business Studies, 42, 1016-1042.*	Further validate that M&A provide opportunities for global diversification.
Carr, C., & Collis, S. (2011, September).	*http://sloanreview.mit. edu/the-magazine/2011-fall/53103/*	Discussed M&A as good global strategy for firms.
Bendeck, Y. M., & Waller, E, R. (2011).	*Journal of Business and Economics Research, 9(8), 41-48.*	Contended that gains in wealth after a bank consolidation may not be as a result of an increased market power generated by the M&A.

Authors	Sources	Summary
Hagendorff, J., & Vallascas, F. (2011).	*Journal of Banking and Finance, 35, 902-915.*	Argue that M&A are not always positive and can increase the default risk of the merged banks.
Allen, F., & Carletti, E. (2010).	*International Review of Finance, 10, 1-26.*	Discussed failure of Lehman Brothers.
Beccalli, E., & Frantz, P. (2013).	*Journal of Financial Services Research, 43, 265-291.*	Argued that bank leaders used M&A to increase the capital positions of the banks.
Schmidt, I. (2011).	*Labour, 68, 238-240.*	Discussed financial bail outs given to banks in the United States.
Croasdale, K., & Stretcher, R. (2011).	*Academy of Banking Studies Journal, 10(2), 67-85.*	Studied the financial crisis in the United States, and lack of financial bail outs for small banks.

Authors	Sources	Summary
Barth, J., & Jahera, J. (2010).	*Journal of Financial Economic Policy, 3, 192-195.*	Discussed the introduction and passing into law of financial reform bill (Dodd-Frank Act).
Prasch, R. E. (2012).	*Journal of Economic Issues, 46, 549-556.*	Contended that the Dodd-Frank Act fails to close the loophole that created the too-big-to-fail status of some financial institutions.
Markham, J. W. (2010).	*Fordham Journal of Corporate and Financial Law, 16, 261-322.*	Questioned whether the new law (Dodd-Frank Act) and regulations will prevent financial crisis from occurring again.
Hargie, O., & Tourish, D. (2012).	*Organizational Studies, 33, 1045-1069.*	Argued that even in failure, a learning opportunity exists in the M&A and should be seized and espoused.

Authors	Sources	Summary
Sperduto, V. (2007).	*(Doctoral dissertation). Available from ProQuest Dissertations and Theses database. (UMI No. 3258978)*	Sperduto (2007) argued that bank leaders focused on the profitability and other benefits of M&A, and lost sight of the human element.
Marks, M. L., & Mirvis, P. H. (2011).	*Journal of Business and Psychology, 26, 161-168.*	Argued that the value of expertise and experience of people in an organization should be deployed to maximize the benefits of the M&A.
Angwin, D., Gomes, E., Mellahi, K., & Peter, E. (2012).	*The International Journal of Human Resource Management, 23, 2874-2900.*	Found that an effective management of human resources is critical for a successful M&A to occur.
Anifowose, B. D., Atiku, O. S., & Genty, K. I. (2011).	*International Journal of Business and Management, 6(11), 67-75.*	Contended that human resources management is a vital part of any M&A process.

Authors	Sources	Summary
Fassin, Y., & Gosselin, D. (2011).	*Journal of Business Ethics, 102, 169-191.*	Found that leaders of merged banks should consider fairness of communication, shareholder activism, and conflicts of interests for Chief Executive Officers (CEOs) as they consider going into M&As.
Ebimobowei, A., & Sophia, J. M. (2011).	*Journal of the Social Sciences, 6, 213-220.*	Found M&A failed to yield the expected result of increasing liquidity, capital adequacy, and achieving stronger corporate governance.
Sagner, J. S. (2012).	*Journal of Corporate Accounting and Finance, 23(2), 21-25.*	Found incompatible management culture, marketing strategies, and excessively optimistic financial projections as reasons some M&A fail.

Authors	Sources	Summary
Addison, R. M., & Lloyd, C. R. (1999).	*Performance Improvement, 38(6), 8-11.*	Found defined vision and mission, cultural consideration, forming a team, contingency plans, effective and timely communication, employee education, rewarding and recognizing success, and monitoring mechanisms as primary factors for successful organizational and performance improvement program necessary for successful M&A.
Adjei-Benin, P., & Sanda, M. (2011).	*Journal of Management and Strategy, 2(2), 28-37.*	Discussed human resources aspect of M&A.
Bhal, K. T., Bhaskar, A. U., & Mishra, B. (2012).	*Global Business Review, 13, 407-419.*	Also discussed human resources aspects of M&A.

Authors	Sources	Summary
Colman, H. L., & Lunnan, R. (2010).	*Journal of Management, 37, 839-860.*	Presented human resources perspectives of M&A.
Kalpic, B. (2008).	*The Journal of Business Strategy, 29(6), 4-13.*	Discussed failure of bank leaders to provide direction during an M&A.
Bhaskar, A. U. (2012)	*Human Resource Management International Digest, 20(2), 22-23.*	Examined human resources aspects of M&A.
Jharkharia, S. (2012).	*International Journal of Aviation Management, 1(4), 293-303.*	Discussed importance of merging the supply chain management of the merging firms to achieve synergy.
Lahovnik, M. (2011).	*Journal for East European Management Studies, 16, 358-370.*	Discussed importance of the sharing of activities and transfer of skills between the acquired and acquiring bank.

Authors	Sources	Summary
Schroeder, H. (2012).	*Strategic HR Review, 11, 272-277.*	Contended that improper integration of cultures of merging organizations can derail the M&A.
Tarba, S., & Weber, Y. (2011).	*International Journal of Organizational Analysis, 19, 202-221.*	Found that the culture of acquired firm may represent a counterculture for the acquiring firm.
Kim, Y. (2011).	*International Journal of Business and Management, 6(4), 49-63.*	Found that culture could negatively affect communication between the acquiring company and the acquired.
Sarala, R, M., & Vaara, E. (2010).	*Journal of International Business Studies, 41, 1365-1390.*	Talked about knowledge transfer benefit of M&A.
Steigner, T., & Sutton, N. K. (2011).	*The Financial Review, 46, 103-125*	Examined if cultural differences between bidder and target banks affect the internationalization benefits of a cross-border merger.

Authors	Sources	Summary
Bjorkman, I., Sarala, R., Stahl, G. K., & Vaara, E. (2010).	*Journal of Management Studies, 49, 1-27.*	Found that organizational and national cultural differences can create social identity issues and at same time provide an opportunity for knowledge transfer.
Awasthy, R., Chandrasekaran, V., & Gupta, R. K. (2011).	*Journal of Indian Business Research, 3, 43-62.*	Showed that effect of culture on organizational performance is significant.
Chen, H., Gu, J., Ke, W., Liu, H., & Wei, K. K..(2010).	*Journal of Operations Management, 28, 372-384.*	Discussed effect of culture on organizational performance.
Teerikangas, S. (2010).	*Journal of Management, 38, 599-639.*	Found that employees can see a merger as an opportunity and not a threat.
Dauber, D. (2012).	*Journal of Cross Cultural Management, 19, 375-398.*	Found that cultural differences are known to have caused the failures of several mergers.

Authors	Sources	Summary
Altinay, L., Riordan, K., & Saunders, M. N. K. (2009).	*The Service Industries Journal, 29, 1359-1375.*	Emphasized importance of effective management of post-merger cultural integration.
Lee, C., Wu, C., & Lee, H. (2009).	*African Journal of Business Management, 3, 695-704.*	Argued that leaders of a merger process should take steps to enhance organizational identity of the acquiring and acquired bank employees.
Al Hawari, M. (2012).	*Journal of Information and Knowledge Management, 11(2), 1-10.*	Found that culture is a primary factor to how employees fit into organizations.
Peloquin, J. (2011).	*(Doctoral dissertation). Available from ProQuest Dissertations and Theses database. (UMI No. 3443646)*	Found that direction of the cultural integration during a merger affects morale of the employees.

Authors	Sources	Summary
Roth, G., & Shook, K. L. (2011).	*Journal of European Industrial Training, 35, 135-153.*	Found that merger leaders should focus on blending cultures instead of changing cultures.
Whitaker, M. K. (2011).	*(Doctoral dissertation). Available from ProQuest Dissertations and Theses database. (UMI No. 3439660)*	Discussed importance of face-to-face communication and mediums that allow giving and receiving feedback for bank employees.
Creasy, T., Stull, M., & Peck, S. (2009).	*http://www. researchgate.net/ publication/259674443_ Understanding_employee- level_dynamics_within_ the_merger_and_ acquisition_process*	Examined determinants of success in blending cultures in merged companies.
Okoro, H. M. (2010).	*(Doctoral dissertation). Available from ProQuest Dissertations and Theses database. (UMI No. 3424825)*	Found that transformational leadership theory emphasizes the importance of organizational culture during organizational change.

Authors	Sources	Summary
do Monte, P. A. (2012).	*The International Journal of Human Resource Management, 23, 1717-1735.*	Used objective behavioral measure variable of job satisfaction to examine job dissatisfaction and employee turnover.
Kaur, G., & Singh, J. (2011)	*International Journal of Commerce and Management, 21, 327-348.*	Discussed importance for business leaders to understand customer satisfaction metrics and the key drivers.
Giessner, S. R., Ullrich, J., & van Dick, R. (2011).	*Social and Personality Psychology Compass, 5, 333-345.*	Found that employees tend to identify more with pre-merger organization than post-merger organization.
Abdullah, M. M. B., & Islam, R. (2012).	*Journal for Global Business Management, 5(4), 285-306.*	Argued that leaders should minimize or eliminate where possible any motivational threats or uncertainties about a merger to enhance employee experience.

Authors	Sources	Summary
Barker, K. J., & Emery, C. R. (2007).	*Team Performance Management, 13, 90-101.*	Studied relationship between job involvement, organizational commitment of employees, and customer satisfaction in a team and non-team environments.
Karunaratne, C., & Wickramasinghe, V. (2009).	*The International Journal of Human Resource Management, 20, 694-715.*	Found that employees were more satisfied with extension merger than collaborative merger.
Roth, G., & Shook, K. L. (2011).	*Journal of European Industrial Training, 35, 135-153*	Discussed need for employee issues to be identified early and addressed.
Adjei-Benin, P., & Sanda, M. (2011).	*Journal of Management and Strategy, 2(2), 28-37.*	Found that employee satisfaction is critical to success of a merger.

To conduct the literature review, I took a thematic approach and examined the following: (a) the history of bank M&A, (b) M&A as a strategy, (c) failed mergers and contributing factors, and (d) the effect of employee satisfaction or dissatisfaction.

History of Bank M&A

The history of bank M&A illustrates prior structures of banks and how M&A became popular growth strategies for bank leaders (Huang & Marquis, 2010). In the 1920s, U.S. commercial bank leaders were able to invest in securities without any restriction (Crawford, 2011). No regulatory framework guided how bank leaders invested in stocks and bonds. No rules or regulations led to immense speculations among banks as bank leaders sought to exploit the stock and bond opportunities from the investment market (Crawford, 2011). The unrestricted investment activities of the banks culminated into the stock market crash of 1929 (Crawford, 2011). Depositors lost monies, and over 9,000 banks failed between 1930 and 1933. Several congressional hearings took place, and finally, the Banking Act of 1933 (Glass-Steagall Act) was passed on June 16, 1933 (Crawford, 2011).

The Banking Act of 1933 restricted financial products banks could offer and geographic locations where banks could operate (Huang & Marquis, 2010). The primary provisions of the act required the separation of investment and commercial banks, restriction of bank deposits for speculation, and deposit insurance, among others. The act sought to prevent conflict of interest between the investment and commercial banks' lines of business and discouraged the inter-state branching of banks (Crawford, 2011). Enacting the act and creating the Federal Deposit Insurance Corporation (FDIC) helped to restore public confidence in the banking sector (Crawford, 2011).

Restrictions on the financial products that banks could offer and the geographic locations where banks could operate fragmented the industry regarding products offered and locations of banks (Huang & Marquis, 2010). In the 1990s, policy makers revisited the restrictions placed on banks. The outcome was the beginning of nationwide branching and universal banking in the United States. However, the Riegle-Neal Interstate Banking and Efficiency Act of 1994 repealed the restrictions on the inter-state branching of banks, and the Gramm-Leach-Bliley Financial Modernization Act of 1999 repealed the Glass-Steagall restrictions (Baker, 2009).

The introduction of the Gramm-Leach-Bliley Financial Modernization Act spurred M&A among banks and integrated the

, and insurance sectors of the economy. Bank leaders moved from creating bank holding companies in states to moving across state lines to merge and acquire other banks (He & Zhao, 2014). The deregulation of the banking industry spurred the consolidation of banks through M&A (Huang & Marquis, 2010). Bank leaders looked at size, growth opportunity, efficiency, and regulatory and supervisory framework as they sought to merge banks (Gaganis, Pasiouras, & Tanna, 2011). Gaganis et al. (2011) examined over 400 commercial banks that underwent M&A and sought to determine why the mergers were necessary. The findings were consistent with the results of past research that strategic M&A generates capital, creates cost efficiency, profitability, and growth opportunities. The history of banks illustrates why M&A are relevant and the issues associated with bank mergers; for instance, social identity issues were not envisioned when bank mergers were initially thought of and created. I sought to address the gap in this study by examining social identity issues associated with M&A.

As the interstate banking and acquisitions were taking hold in the United States in the 1990s, cross-border M&A were becoming common among different countries in the European Union (EU; Boateng & Uddin, 2011). The bank leaders moved across national borders to take advantage of perceived synergy in merging with target banks (Ghobadian, Hitt, Kling, O'Regan & Weitzel, 2014). The era of liberalization, deregulation, and advances in technology combined to change the financial landscape, and the competition between banks and non-bank financial institutions rose to a new level (Beck, Levine, & Levkov, 2010). New distribution channels and product innovations led to new opportunities and new competitors, so bank leaders looked for ways to survive or dominate the competition and turned to M&As as a strategy (Huang & Marquis, 2010). Bank executives merged banks to achieve synergy and improve management of the acquired institution (Huyghebaert & Luypaert, 2013).

For bank leaders, the deregulation of banks created immense opportunities and fierce competition (He & Zhao, 2014). Leaders of large banks were able to offer lucrative traditional and non-traditional products that smaller banks were unable to offer, so bank leaders saw M&A as an avenue for growth and expansion to allow banks to offer more lucrative product mix (He & Zhao, 2014). The strong economy at the time allowed leaders to generate high levels of profitability and capital positions, and bank leaders embarked on M&A to strengthen their competitive positions (Crawford, 2011). This review of the history of banks showed that bank M&A became necessary at a certain point, but bank merger pioneers did not foresee the attendant issues associated with bank mergers. I sought to address this gap through the current research.

M&As as a Strategy

President Clinton signed the Riegle-Neal Interstate Banking and Efficiency Act of 1994 into law on September 29, 1994. As a result, policy makers created an environment that allowed bank leaders to operate and compete at levels considered impossible in the past (Beck, Levine, & Levkov, 2010). Provisions of the act gave national bank leaders the authority to own branches across the United States by opening new branch offices or acquisitioning other bank branches (Beck et al., 2010). New opportunities resulted in interstate banking and branching in the United States (Heiney, 2011).

Several bank leaders resorted to M&A as growth strategies (Phillips & Zhdanov, 2013). Malul, Meydani, and Shoham (2012) found that bank leaders and managers gained more market share and maximized profit through M&A. M&A also became a way to eliminate operating inefficiencies and reduce processing expenses for banks (Assaf, Barros, & Ibiwoye, 2012; Baker, 2009; Bernard, Fuentelsaz, & Gomez, 2010). While bank leaders were taking advantage of the deregulated environment, effective preparations were not made to adequately integrate employees who were acquired in the M&A process. As a result, no adequate strategies were implemented to address the social identity issues that arose with M&A.

Taking advantage of economies of scale is a primary driver of bank mergers in the United States (Wheelock & Wilson, 2012). Wheelock and Wilson (2012) conducted their study using local polynomial estimators and data obtained from United States banks from 1984 to 2006. The researchers found that the trend for banks to merge to take advantage of economies of scale would continue unless government institutions intervened.

In another study used to examine M&A as a strategy, Lambkin and Muzellec (2010) found that the acquirer company (with the stronger brand recognition than the acquired company) should consider renaming the acquired company to bear the same name as the parent company. Renaming the acquired company can convey to the market that ownership and management have changed for the acquired company. However, renaming the acquired company may also alienate the customer base established by the acquired company, so individuals implementing the merger process should be mindful of the potential alienation that could occur. If the acquiring company has higher brand recognition, Lambkin and Muzellec concluded that the acquired company should assume the name of the acquiring company. The researchers posited that following this strategy could help bank leaders achieve successful M&A.

Hoberg and Phillips (2010) also examined why bank M&A are necessary by investigating firms that merged to take advantage of similar, but unique, product offerings. Hoberg and Phillips found that firms with similar product market language are more suited to enter into merger transactions. M&A in competitive product markets yield increased stock returns and growth for the firms. If targets are unique from acquirer's rivals, stock returns and growth will be high because acquiring firms take advantage of the product differentiation opportunity presented by M&As (Hoberg & Phillips, 2010).

Successful implementation of M&A provides the opportunity for knowledge transfer between the merging firms (Azan & Sutter, 2010; Holland & Salama, 2010). Using the merger between the Roche Consumer Health division and Bayer as a case study, Azan and Sutter (2010) examined M&A from a knowledge transfer perspective. The researchers explored the knowledge variable in the Hellenic Post-Merger Integration (PMI) of the two companies, and they investigated whether the stakeholders considered knowledge transfer as a key driver in deciding whether to undertake the merger. The researchers conducted the research six months after the conclusion of the merger process and found that knowledge transfer and synergy were the reasons for the merger. Bank leaders tend to focus on the benefits of

M&A and overlook the strategy necessary to accomplish successful M&A. Lack of specific strategies aimed at overcoming issues (e.g., social identity problems that arise after M&A) exacerbate the failure rates of M&A (Baker, 2009).

Examining M&A as a strategy is important to give insight into the primary reasons bank leaders chose to merge banks and important issues left unaddressed in their decision process. In this context, Fethi, Kumbhakar, Lozano-Vivas, and Shaban (2011) examined the effectiveness of the merger processes in European banks from 1998 to 2004. Fethi et al. used the stochastic cost frontier approach to estimate the efficiency in profitability and examined any improvements in cost, return on assets, and return on equity to validate these cost benefits as good reasons for undertaking an M&A. Results of the study indicated improved cost efficiencies from M&As. Evripidou (2012) found improved cost efficiency, economies of scale, and market power as the reasons for mergers. Evripidou examined pre-merger and post-merger data from two merged airline companies. Results showed decreased post-merger systematic risk and improved cost efficiencies. In contrast, Behr and Heid (2011) studied German banks that underwent M&A from 1995 to 2000. Behr and Heid examined the effects of the mergers on profitability and cost efficiency but found a neutral effect of mergers on both accounts. The contrasting results present opportunity for future research.

Erel, Liao, and Weisbach (2012) analyzed a sample of 56,978 cross-border mergers from 1990 to 2007 for evidence of increased valuation after merger. Results indicated that the increased valuation of merged banks could be the primary motivator of a merger. Erel et al. also found that firms in countries with booming stock markets tend to be the acquirers in merger deals. Firms from countries with stronger currencies also tend to be the acquirers, and firms from weaker-performing economies are targets for merger deals (Erel et al., 2012). Examining why M&A are necessary, Jog and Zhu (2012) studied large samples of M&A data from emerging countries. Results indicated that target firms benefit from cross-border M&A and cross-border M&A results to reduced risks for the target firm and increases the stock valuation. This assertion was further validated in other studies (Bhuyan, Ng, & Vaziri, 2010; Goto, Nogata, & Uchida, 2011;

Olowe, 2011). Acquiring banks benefit from increased value resulting from the announcement of M&A. Bhuyan et al. (2010) examined valuation effect of the merger announcement on banks based in the United States and Europe from 2004 to 2010. The researchers used traditional event study method to conduct the study, and results showed 0.3% and 0.8% increases in wealth valuation for merged banks in the United States and Europe, respectively (Bhuyan et al., 2010).

If acquiring banks have weak governance, equity values of banks, on average, do not display positive returns upon the announcement (Piskula, 2011). Using the commercially sold governance index from Institutional Shareholder Services, Piskula (2011) measured the governance strength of several banks involved in M&As. Piskula selected banks that were involved in M&A from 2001 to 2006 from the comprehensive Thomson Reuters SDC merger database. Upon announcing M&A, inferior stock market reactions occurred in banks with weak governance, and positive reactions were evident for banks with strong governance (Piskula, 2011). Value generation from announcing mergers is not evenly common across countries (Alexandridis, Petmezas, & Travlos, 2010). According to Alexandridis et al. (2010), acquirers in competitive takeover markets (e.g., United States, United Kingdom [UK], and Canada) benefit from these announcements, but acquirers from less competitive takeover countries do not benefit as much from these announcements. Instead, acquirers from less competitive takeover countries benefit more from the low premiums paid for acquisitions than they do from the benefits from merger announcements. Acquirers' share-to-share offers are, at worst, neutral in value generation for the shareholders. Alexandridis et al. concluded that acquirers and targets benefit from M&A.

In the study of the Royal Bank of Scotland (RBS), Muhammad (2011) found that the merger deal failed to improve the financial performance of the bank. Muhammad used twenty vital accounting ratios to analyze the financial performance of the bank from 2006 to 2009. The researcher examined the profitability, liquidity, assets management, leverage, and cash flow positions of RBS. Results indicated that M&A failed to improve financial performance of the bank. However, the literature review revealed that bank leaders undertake merger ventures to gain more operating efficiency, enhanced market power, improved risk diversification, and heightened economies of scale and scope, but these goals are not always achieved (Buch, Koch, & Koetter, 2013).

Despite above stated benefits of M&A, Liargovas and Repousis (2011) contend that M&A do not create wealth. The researchers used the event study method to examine the Greek banking sector from 1996 to 2009 and investigated twenty financial ratios in the Greek banking sector. Results of the study rejected the semi-strong form of the Efficient Market Hypothesis from the Athens stock exchange and indicated that operating performance did not improve after M&A. The position of Liargovas and Repousis were validated through another study (Samet, 2010). Samet (2010) studied a merged Tunis bank and found no added value resulting from M&A. Samet studied the merger by takeover of the Banque de Developpement de l'Economie Tunisienne and the Banque Nationale du Developpement Touristique by the Societe Tunisienne des Banques. Samet examined the ratio of return on sales (or net income ratio), ratios of return on assets, and equity. In each case, the ratios recorded lower return after M&A. Samet concluded that, in the short- and mid-terms, no values were created. Harada and Ito (2011) found that M&A do not create incremental value for the merged banks; they calculated and analyzed the distance to default (DD) of large Japanese banks to determine if M&A made merging banks financially stronger. Results of the study indicated that merged banks inherit the financial wellbeing of the merging banks. For instance, if two weak banks merge, the result will be a combined weak bank. In some cases, the researchers found that merged banks experienced negative DD. From 1990 to 2005, the goal of the mergers in Japan was to prevent big bank failures instead of achieving cost efficiencies and other documented reasons for M&As (Harada & Ito, 2011).

Chaudhary, Kaushik, and Sinha (2010) examined the pre and post-merger efficiency of Indian banks that were involved in mergers from 2002 to 2008. The researchers used the ratio analysis approach and a nonparametric Wilcoxon signed-rank test to evaluate the performance of the banks. Results of the study indicated a significant correlation between financial performance and M&A. Chaudhary et al. concluded that M&A generate value for the acquiring firms. The aim of most bank mergers in the United States is increase in shareholder value, but Mehrotra, Spronk, Steenbeek, and van Schaik (2011) found that mergers in Japan often do not result in increases in shareholder value. Mehrotra et al. studied 91 mergers in Japan from 1982 to 2003 and found that mergers in Japan are determined by the demands of creditors, whereas in the United States, shareholder interests are the primary drivers of M&A. The differing research findings perhaps present an opportunity for further research.

M&A as a strategy have created competitive advantages for banks that had the resources to take advantage of the opportunities (Mylonakis, 2006). Bernile, Lyandres, and Zhdanov (2011) examined why firms embark on horizontal mergers. Bernile et al. evaluated empirical evidence based on parametric and semi-parametric regression analysis and found that motivators for undertaking M&A include strong competitive interaction among firms and perceived low cost for restructuring and merging the firms. Bank leaders acquire securities' firms to bolster market share (Papaioannou, 2011). M&A have also become a viable tool for internationalization of banks (Amine, Khan, Uddin, & Zaman, 2011). Small banks facing financial difficulties sought strategically to merge with the bank that offered them the best synergy (Baker, 2009; Mili & Sahut, 2011). Solvency, size of the firm, and efficiency levels are primary determinants of acquisition opportunity (García-Suaza & Gómez-González, 2010). Successful implementation of M&A provides opportunities for global diversification that attracts favorable valuation for the merged firms (Hankir, Rauch, & Umber, 2011; Li, Qiu, & Wan, 2011). M&A are good global strategies for some firms, but for others, a regional strategy may be more favorable (Carr & Collis, 2011). Bendeck and Waller (2011) found that gains in wealth after a bank consolidation may not result from increased market power generated by M&A. However, M&A are not always positive and can increase the default risk of the merged banks (Hagendorff & Vallascas, 2011).

The financial crises of 2008 brought a change of events in the financial service industry. The crisis reached its height with the failure of Lehman Brothers in September 2008 (Allen & Carletti, 2010). According to Allen and Carletti (2010), the crisis was engineered by the unrealistic inflated valuation of the real estate market in the United States and other countries, loose monetary policy (which made credit cheap and easy to access), and global imbalance in the financial markets. Subprime lending, weak regulatory structures, and high leverage in the banking sector exacerbated these issues. As the crisis mounted, the financial industry experienced liquidity squeeze. With the tightening of credit, banks began to experience higher levels of delinquencies from loan customers. This situation put pressure on banks for liquidity because the banks relied on paying loan customers to meet obligations to the depositors. Consequently, according to Beccalli and Frantz (2012), bank leaders sought to increase their capital positions and turned to M&A to stay in business. Bank leaders also merged banks to save failing banks from collapsing and causing more harm to the financial system. As the financial crises heightened, the financial regulators increased the pace at which merger requests were approved to abate the effect of failing banks on the economy of the United States.

Bank leaders diversify risks and increase market penetration via M&A. The goal is to eliminate competition and strengthen their positions in the marketplace by increasing presence in more locations and provision of more diverse products. Acquiring more financial institutions to increase market penetration and eliminate competition did not always work out as it was initially envisioned. The banking crises continued and reached a height in 2009. As a result, several major banks that acquired other financial institutions received financial bailouts from the federal government (Schmidt, 2011).

The Treasury Department of the U.S. government explained that allowing the banks to fail could have a catastrophic effect on the economy of the United States because of the size of the banks in question (Shull, 2010). The smaller banks, however, did not receive financial bailouts, so they continued to bear the financial burden of the financial crisis through increased assessment fees, costs of funds, and regulation compliance (Croasdale & Stretcher, 2011). In an effort to prevent future financial crises, the financial reform bill, otherwise known as the Dodd-Frank Act, was passed and signed into law in the United States on July 21, 2010 (Barth & Jahera, 2010). According to Prasch (2012), this act ignored the loophole that created the too-big-to-fail status of some financial institutions. Prasch contended that some financial institutions still engage in aggressive, risky ventures and are over-leveraged. Prasch concluded that additional steps should be taken to prevent any financial institution from being too big to fail. It remains uncertain whether the new law and regulations will prevent any future financial crisis (Markham, 2010; Vives, 2011).

According to Hargie and Tourish (2012), bank leaders testified to the banking crisis inquiry of the Treasury Committee of the U.K. House of Commons in 2009. The leaders' strategy was to absolve them or minimize their responsibility for any wrongdoing. The bank leaders argued that the actions they took were the norms and generally accepted practices of the industry; they also argued that they had no complete control of the events, and were seemingly passive observers. Hargie and Tourish found that bank leaders' positions were not credible. The authors concluded that the bank leaders muddled the public discourse and potentially jeopardized opportunities for learning from failure. Hargie and Tourish argued that even in failure, a learning opportunity exists in M&A and should be seized and espoused.

Sperduto (2007) examined opportunities for M&A and found that bank leaders focus on the benefits the mergers bring regarding improved profitability and increased strength in the marketplace; however, the leaders paid less attention to the human elements of the transaction in the form of employees who would be acquired in the process. The value of expertise and experience of people in an organization should be deployed to maximize the benefits of the M&A (Marks & Mirvis, 2011). Bank leaders fail to recognize the importance of the acquired employees' roles to help realize the goal of the merger. The effective integration of the acquired employees is necessary to avoid or minimize social identity issues and achieve the stated objectives of M&A. Angwin, Gomes, Mellahi, and Peter (2012) found that an effective management of human resources is critical for successful M&A to occur. The authors conducted the research in Nigeria by interviewing primary informants in the mergers, and results indicated that human resources remain a thorny issue, which has the potential to derail any merger if not approached and managed strategically and effectively. Human resources management is a vital part of any M&A process, but often ignored (Anifowose, Atiku, & Genty, 2011).

Some of the studies examined above highlighted the benefits of M&A. Others contend that M&A do not create wealth and do not add value to the merged organization (Liargovas & Repousis, 2011; Samet, 2010). This review of literature also revealed that proponents of M&A often do not prepare for the social identity issues that may arise after M&A, and as a result, the goals of several M&A are not attained (Baker, 2009). In this study, I seek to add to the existing literature about the importance of preparing for the social identity issues associated with M&A.

Failed Mergers: Contributing Factors

Several factors have contributed to M&A failures to achieve their anticipated goals. Leaders of merged banks should consider fairness of communication, shareholder activism, and conflicts of interests for Chief Executive Officers (CEO) as bank leaders delve into M&A (Fassin & Gosselin, 2011). Fassin and Gosselin (2011) used Fortis Group's acquisition of the Algemene Bank Nederland (ABN) and the Amsterdamsche and Rotterdamsche Banks (AMRO) as the case study to determine why mergers fail. Fortis was successful in five previous mergers, but the financial powerhouse failed one year after acquiring ABN and AMRO. The researchers found that the financial crises from 2008 to 2009 eroded trust in the financial industry and that Fortis was in the middle of it. Fortis was reputable for its leadership in the corporate social responsibility (CSR) arena, but conflicts existed between the CSR policies of Fortis and the 2008–2009 realities in the financial industry. As a result, risks were not correctly evaluated.

Ebimobowei and Sophia (2011) examined the M&A that occurred in the Nigerian banking industry. Using the exploratory research method, the researchers sought to determine the efficacy of the wave of mergers that reduced the number of banks in Nigeria from 89 to 25 banks. Ebimobowei and Sophia found that the mergers did not achieve their stated objectives. The stated goals of the mergers were to increase liquidity, capital adequacy, and achieve stronger corporate governance. The aftermath of the mergers resulted in more troubled banks and not stronger and better-capitalized banks, which was anticipated before the M&A. Ebimobowei and Sophia found that corruption, fraud, and insider abuses were some reasons the mergers failed.

Sagner (2012) found that incompatible management culture, marketing strategies, and excessively optimistic financial projections are reasons some M&A fail. Individuals implementing M&A should examine the corporate cultures of the merging firms and align them to facilitate synergy. Also, marketing strategies should be realigned to reflect the vision and direction of the new company, and merger leaders must refrain from making overly optimistic financial projections and avoid setting unattainable goals. Sagner found that although account receivables and inventory are the most important and critical components in M&A, they often do not attract the attention of investment bankers, accountants, or attorneys who administer M&A. Sagner recommended that account receivables and inventory should be documented accurately to enhance M&A success.

Employees of merged banks should be informed in a timely manner. Well-timed communication can help eliminate or minimize speculation and gossip (Addison & Lloyd, 1999). Addison and Lloyd (1999) found that the following are primary factors for successful M&A: vision and mission, cultural consideration, teamwork, contingency plans, effective and timely communications, employee education, rewards and recognitions of success, and mechanism monitoring.

The human resources aspects of M&A should be addressed as seriously as are the expected financial returns (Adjei-Benin & Sanda, 2011; Bhal, Bhaskar, & Mishra, 2012). M&A leaders focus on meeting the financial returns expected by investors and emphasize cost cutting, but in the process, leaders may treat employees and payroll as part of the cost elements instead of important drivers of the company's success. Economic, financial, and strategic factors drive mergers, but the human resources component should be incorporated into the strategy (Bhal, Bhaskar, & Mishra, 2012; Bhaskar, 2012;

Colman & Lunnan, 2010). The increase in market penetration and power, effect of poor vision, inability to execute or achieve synergy, culture issues between merging companies, and employee dissatisfaction should also be considered.

Kalpic (2008) found that bank leaders sometimes embark on M&A efforts to benefit from the competitive advantage and profits that can result from mergers. In the process, bank leaders fail to define the direction of the new company; lack of vision and direction keep the merged companies from optimizing the combined strength. Managers of M&A should define and communicate the vision and mission of the new firm (Addison & Lloyd, 1999).

Bank leaders who implement M&A must design a clear plan that will integrate the managerial executives, finances, and systems of the merging banks (Mylonakis, 2006). The supply chain management of merging firms should be integrated to achieve synergy (Jharharia, 2012). Execution and success of M&A can be enhanced by ensuring that activities are shared and skills are transferred between acquired banks and acquiring banks (Lahovnik, 2011). The integration process must include trust, communication, transfer of teaching, and fairness of treatment, but improperly integrating cultures of the merging organizations can derail M&As (Schroeder, 2012). Integrating these primary functions can ensure that new companies are unified.

The culture of the acquired firm may represent a counterculture from the acquiring firm (Tarba & Weber, 2011) and could negatively affect communication between the companies (Kim, 2011). For international mergers, merging banks should pay attention to national and cultural differences and the potential for knowledge transfer (Sarala & Vaara, 2010; Steigner & Sutton, 2011). Steigner and Sutton (2011) examined if cultural differences between bidder and target banks affect the internationalization benefits of a cross-border merger. Steigner and Sutton found that cultural differences affect the performance of bidder banks after M&As. Organizational and national cultural differences can create social identity issues and can provide an opportunity for knowledge transfer (Bjorkman, Sarala, Stahl, & Vaara, 2010). Cultural differences are viewed as dividers between employees of acquiring companies and employees of acquired companies, but these differences also provide opportunities for cultural learning (Bjorkman et al., 2010). Bjorkman et al. argued that the effects of organizational culture and national culture are different. The authors contended that organizational culture may be the source of the social identity disruption, but national culture provides a real opportunity for cultural exchange and learning.

Past research results have shown that culture significantly affects organizational performance (Awasthy, Chandrasekaran, & Gupta, 2011; Chen, Gu, Ke, Liu, Ke, & Wei, 2010). Awasthy et al. (2011) illustrated this by studying the Indian public sector bank to understand employees' experiences in a top-down culture change. The researchers used a qualitative case study approach to seek and understand the event of culture change in a top-down system. Results indicated that the leadership of any merger should approach culture change issues strategically, but bank leaders often ignore the importance of proper integration of cultures between the merging banks (Tarba & Weber, 2011). This situation creates tension between the employees of the merging banks because employees wonder whether they will retain their titles and positions (Baker, 2009). Employees from acquired banks may resent acquiring banks because employees may be treated unfairly if they do not follow the objectives and stated purpose of the M&A (Mylonakis, 2006). Mylonakis examined how bank employees perceive bank M&A and investigated how it affects employees' personal and professional careers. Results indicated that bank employees felt threatened by M&A. Findings also showed that leaders and managers of M&A should be sensitive to employees' experiences during the merger to ensure that employees do not see the merger as a threat to their personal or professional wellbeing.

Teerikangas (2010) studied eight acquisitions by Finnish multinationals and found that employees can see the merger as an opportunity and not a threat. For instance, six out of the eight cases studied showed that if employees are motivated and do not feel anxious or uncertain about the merger, employees' reactions to the merger will be positive. Acquirer companies should demonstrate consistent and positive intentions, and the target company should reinforce a strategic and positive response to the merger. Target companies should proactively promote the acquisition success and demonstrate the need to be acquired (Teerikangas, 2010).

Cultural differences have been known to cause the failures of several mergers (Dauber, 2012). The importance of effective management of post-merger cultural integration cannot be over-emphasized (Altinay, Riordan, & Saunders, 2009). Altinay et al. (2009) used a mixed-methods design to examine the importance of effective cultural integration post-merger. In the study, Altinay et al. identified important factors necessary for effective management of post-merger cultural integration. The researchers identified the following as vital components of achieving successful post-merger cultural integration: strong leadership, open and honest communication, and pre-merger culture assessment.

Leaders of merger processes should take steps to enhance the organizational identity of acquiring and acquired bank employees (Lee, Lee, & Wu, 2009). Lee et al. (2009) examined factors that influence employees' organizational identities after M&A, from the perspectives of acquirers and acquired bank employees. The researchers selected four acquiring banks and four acquired banks and used convenience sampling to obtain 261 completed questionnaires. One hundred and thirty five responses were obtained from the acquirer banks, and 126 responses were obtained from the acquired banks. Using multi-regression analysis, the researchers found that trust and procedural justice influence the employees' perception of organizational identity. Bank leaders should be aware of factors that influence organizational identity as they execute and lead future bank mergers.

Culture is a primary factor of how employees fit into organizations (Al Hawari, 2012). Improper integration of merging banks' cultures can create a cultural collision between the two banks, resulting in employee dissatisfaction. Idle and Speculand (2012) examined the factors responsible for the failures at Mid Staffs (a general hospital in England) and the collapse of Lehman Brothers bank in the United States. The researchers found that the weak management culture was a primary factor of the colossal failures. Directions of the cultural integrations during mergers affect the morale of the employees

(Peloquin, 2011), so merger leaders should focus on blending cultures instead of changing cultures (Roth & Shook, 2011).

When employees are engaged through face-to-face communication and media that allow giving and receiving feedback, employees' dedication will most likely increase (Whitaker, 2011). Whitaker (2011) examined how cultures affect post-mergers. Whitaker found that culture must not be allowed to emerge on its own after M&A; instead, leaders of mergers should proactively influence culture to ensure that preferred cultural dimensions emerge post-merger. If the culture is not strategically implemented pre- and post-merger, top talents may leave, and employee productivity will decline. Using a quantitative study approach, Whitaker examined the preferred cultural dimensions of non-managerial employees post-merger. Whitaker used the Organizational Cultural Assessment Instrument to interpret and analyze the data obtained to assess the preferred cultural dimensions. Results indicated that employees prefer cultural dimensions post-merger. Leaders of mergers should strive to achieve the preferred cultural dimensions post-merger to enhance the success of M&As (Whitaker, 2011).

Creasy, Peck, and Stull (2010) examined what determines success in blending cultures in merged companies. The researchers studied the employee level factors, such as job satisfaction, organizational citizenship, and perception of management. They also tested for managerial guided, direct, and indirect effects of culture on employee level dynamics. Results indicated that cultural identity is relevant to employees and critical for M&A to succeed.

Transformational leadership theory emphasizes the importance of organizational culture during organizational change (Okoro, 2010). Okoro (2010) used quantitative correlation and regression analysis to examine if any relationship exists between organizational culture and organizational performance. Okoro found evidence of relationships among cultural traits, such as mission, involvement, consistency, adaptability, and organizational performance measures. The organizational performance measures identified in this study are employee commitment, job satisfaction, and employee retention. Inadequate cultural integration during M&A could result in merger failure and decreased organizational performance. Okoro found that the lack of employee commitment, reduction in job satisfaction, and increase in employee turnover contributed to unsuccessful mergers. Organizational cultural differences could hinder organizational performance, so leaders of merger transactions should approach culture strategically and not as a short-term issue.

Employee Satisfaction or Dissatisfaction

Unsatisfied employees deliver unsatisfactory service to customers. In a study of selected Indian banks in the cities of Punjab and Chandigarh, Kaur and Singh (2011) examined factors that affect customer satisfaction. Kaur and Singh used questionnaires to collect data from a sample of 456 respondents and used a multiple regression approach to analyze the data obtained. Results indicated that the following affect customer satisfaction: employee responsiveness, appearance of intangibles, social responsibility, service innovation, positive word-of-mouth, competence, and reliability (Kaur & Singh, 2011). Business leaders should understand customer satisfaction metrics and the primary drivers (Kaur & Singh, 2011). Understanding customer satisfaction metrics will enable leaders to develop appropriate and adaptive strategies to maximize the opportunity presented by M&A (Kaur & Singh, 2011).

Do Monte (2012) used the objective behavioral measure of job satisfaction to examine the job dissatisfaction and employee turnover in the Brazilian labor market. The researcher also used econometric techniques, such as multinomial, to determine if job satisfaction is a good predictor of employee turnover. Results from do Monte's study indicated that the job satisfaction of employees reduces employee turnover.

Employees tend to identify more with the pre-merger organization than they do with the post-merger organization (Giessner, Ullrich, & van Dick, 2011). Leaders and managers of merger transactions should be sensitive to employees' experiences during the merger process. Leaders should minimize or eliminate any motivational threats or uncertainties about the merger to enhance employees' experiences (Abdullah & Islam, 2012). Part of the goal in merging should be to ensure that employees identify more with the post-merger organization than they do with the pre-merger organization (Giessner et al., 2011). Barker and Emery (2007) studied relationships between job involvement, organizational commitment of employees, and customer satisfaction in team and non-team environments. The researchers used the field design method to examine the service departments of 40 automobile dealerships in different places. Results showed a direct relationship between the organizational commitment and job involvement of customer contact with employees and customer satisfaction. Job involvement of employees is significantly correlated to profit, productivity, and customer satisfaction (Barker & Emery, 2007).

M&A can create major trauma for employees of the acquired bank and employees of the acquiring bank (Kusstatscher, Sinkovics, & Zagelmeyer, 2011). This trauma can lead to attitudinal and productivity problem and valued employees may start to leave the bank (Baker, 2009; Barker & Emery, 2007). Karunaratne and Wickramasinghe (2009) examined employee experiences after M&A and sought employees' perspectives and experiences on people management post-merger. The researchers selected two banks in Sri Lanka that experienced extension and collaborative mergers, respectively. One hundred and nine employees from the banks responded to the questionnaires, and the researchers found that employees were more satisfied with the extension merger than they were with the collaborative merger. The findings also indicated that age, gender, and marital status were factors to determine employees' satisfaction, and age was the most influential than was any factor. The inquiry was carried out further in this study by focusing on roles of additional factors, such as race, job level, gender, and level of education on employee satisfaction after M&A.

The financial crises from 2007 to 2009 affected the working conditions of bank employees and, in some cases, resulted in employee layoffs (Baker, 2009). Employees could start to search for new jobs instead of staying focused and committed to their current employment. Baker (2009) found that sometimes, employees who go through mergers may question the motives of the leaders, which can affect how employees perform their jobs. According to Baker, evidence of this could be seen in employees' refusals to move to different locations, decreased productivity, resignations, stealing from companies, and disloyalty to the organization. The change management aspect of M&A is critical and affects the employees immensely, so employees wonder how much change to expect, when it will happen, and how long it will take. This confusion can create dissatisfaction that could affect performance. During financial crises, employees of distressed banks present higher levels of anxiety than do employees of non-distressed banks, so employee issues should be identified and addressed early (Roth & Shook, 2011).

Baker (2009) found that employees experience mixed emotions ranging from negative emotions of shock, disbelief, anger, and helplessness to positive emotions of hope, excitement, and high expectations about the future after M&A. Baker raised human resources issues, which were further examined in Adjei-Benin and Sanda (2011). Adjei-Benin and Sanda examined relationships among employee satisfaction, employee productivity, and performance of the merged firm. The study showed that organizational leaders, while in pursuit of new and emerging markets, encounter several human resources issues. Leaders should develop a two-way communication strategy and institute participatory approaches in job redesign processes to help appropriately and effectively manage the human factors involved in the merger process (Adjei-Benin & Sanda, 2011). The researchers discussed and found that employee satisfaction is critical to the success of mergers (Adjei-Benin & Sanda, 2011).

TRANSITION AND SUMMARY

Section 1 introduced the study examining the job satisfaction of bank employees after M&A. As discussed, satisfied employees positively affect the outcome of mergers (Baker, 2009). Demographic variables, such as job tenure, job level, age, level of education, and gender can play significant roles to determine the post-merger job satisfaction of employees (Baker, 2009). The need to understand and manage employee satisfaction cannot be overemphasized. Section 2 includes the details of the research project and the steps used to design, develop, and conduct the research.

CHAPTER 2

The Project

In this section, I presented the details and the steps I took to conduct the study. It includes the identification or location of participants, role of researcher, data collection process and tools used, method used, and how I analyzed data. I also discussed the ethical compliance, reliability and validity of tools, and data security.

PURPOSE STATEMENT

The purpose of this quantitative research study was to examine factors that influence the exit of top-performing employees, including leaders from the banks after the M&A from the perspectives of job tenure, job title, race, age, gender, or level of education of the bank employees. Using a quantitative descriptive design, I examined the effects of the stated factors on satisfaction levels post-merger. Job tenure, job title, race, age, gender, and level of education were the independent variables and job satisfaction was the dependent variable.

The specific population group studied was bank employees who experienced M&A between 2006 and 2009. I obtained the sample of participants from Sunshine Bank (pseudonym). Sunshine Bank's employees work in several different states in the United States. For the research to be more manageable in scope, I conducted the study on employees in Bucks, Delaware, Montgomery, and Philadelphia counties of Pennsylvania.

Bank executives could use the information obtained from the research to manage future mergers in manners that will minimize or eliminate employee anxieties, turnover and job losses. If more mergers are effectively managed and successful, more employees may be retained. The employed individuals could support their families, and perhaps contribute to building better communities.

ROLE OF THE RESEARCHER

I was an objective observer and neither participated nor influenced the study. I was a banker from 1998 to 2012. During this period, I worked as vice president (VP) of consumer banking for a leading bank in the United States and experienced at least three different bank mergers. I reminded myself that I must remain neutral and not allow my personal experience to interfere with the research in any way.

To contact participants, I obtained the telephone numbers of the bank's branches and other offices by searching online for the listed locations of the bank in Bucks, Delaware, Montgomery, and Philadelphia counties of Pennsylvania. I called each branch in the stated locations and obtained the e-mail address of the manager at each location. I sent e-mail to the branch managers and managers of other lines of businesses surveyed (see Appendix B). I requested the managers to complete the survey by clicking on a link and forward the e-mails to the rest of the employees to complete the survey.

I asked and obtained the copyright permission from the Job Descriptive Index (JDI) Research Group, Department of Psychology, Bowling Green State University to use the Abridged Job in General (AJIG) questionnaire to collect data. The JDI Research Group, Bowling Green State University, owns the copyright for the AJIG. A copy of the permission from Bowling Green State University is included as Appendix D.

PARTICIPANTS

I searched online and obtained the telephone number to the office of the CEO of Sunshine Bank (pseudonym). I called the office and obtained the e-mail address of the CEO. I also obtained the telephone numbers of the branches from online sources, called branches and obtained the e-mail addresses of the branch managers. I sent an e-mail to the CEO of Sunshine Bank, requesting the participation of the CEO and employees of the bank in Delaware, Philadelphia, Montgomery, and Bucks counties of Pennsylvania (see Appendix E). I e-mailed each branch manager and requested them to complete the survey and forward the e-mail to the rest of the employees to complete the survey. I explained the purpose of the study to the participants (see Appendix B), and the expectation was that the participating employees would see how the study could benefit them and respond truthfully. The questionnaire was framed to avoid any question that may reveal the identity of the participant. The privacy of the participants and data obtained were protected as provided in SurveyMonkey® confidentiality and security policy (see Appendix F). I attached a copy of the Informed Consent Form (see Appendix G) to each e-mail sent to participants and have opt-out option for participants. I have the collected data in locked container and will destroy them after 5 years.

I selected the participants through purposeful sampling. Purposeful sampling method is most appropriate when participants who meet known standards or conditions are required for a study (Krishnaswamy & Satyaprasad, 2010). The participants needed for the current study were the bank employees who work for Sunshine Bank, in Bucks, Delaware, Montgomery, and Philadelphia counties of Pennsylvania, and experienced M&A between 2006 and 2009. The use of purposeful sampling increased the chance to select bank employees with the required criteria.

Based on the information I obtained from calling the branches, Sunshine bank has 55 branches in Bucks, Delaware, Montgomery, and Philadelphia counties of Pennsylvania, with an average number of eight employees per branch. The response rate for this study was 49.3%, based on 217 respondents obtained from a population of 440 employees. Using G*Power 3.1.7 software (Buchner, Erdfelder, Faul, & Lang, 2009), I performed an initial a priori power-analysis to determine the sample size necessary for the full six-way ANOVA (Fixed effects, special, main effects and interactions) with numerator $df = 2$ and number of groups = 96, with an effect size of 0.35 (f) and a power of 0.80, at alpha level of 0.05. The result of the power analysis was $N = 107$. This result indicated that a sample size of 107 respondents was needed for the full ANOVA model with the minimum number of levels per variable; gender (2 levels), age (2 levels), race (3 levels), education (2 levels), job level (2 levels), and tenure (2 levels). No participant was able to access the survey without first reading the Informed Consent Form (see Appendix G).

RESEARCH METHOD AND DESIGN

I used a quantitative descriptive method and obtained survey responses from bank employees to examine if job tenure, job level, age, gender, race, or level of education affected their job satisfaction levels after the M&A. I requested the participants to click on the link to complete the survey. The participants completed questionnaires and I collected the data within 7 days. Questionnaires are effective tools to collect data for a quantitative study (Stacy, 2010). I obtained responses from participants across levels of employment at the bank in the stated locations in Pennsylvania to ensure balanced responses, regarding content and representation.

Method

The quantitative research method was used to conduct the study. The quantitative research method provides the means for explaining phenomena by collecting numerical data and analyzing the data through a mathematically or statistically based method (Muijs, 2004). I collected survey data from bank employees who experienced M&A, and applied statistical measures to analyze the data. In a quantitative study, what is measured or sought is known. I collected the data, and analyzed them to test the hypotheses. Researcher bias is usually minimal or absent in a quantitative study (Muijs, 2004). Qualitative data are not usually numerical (Muijs, 2004). Qualitative method revolves more around the quality and texture of participants' experiences (Willig, 2013). Qualitative researchers do not seek to measure particular attributes in a large number of people; rather the researchers focus on exploring details of the phenomenon or experience (Willig, 2013). Qualitative researchers focus on providing detailed human experiences of particular cases by engaging in close study of those cases (Beck & Polit, 2010). Given that I collected numerical data and used statistical measures to analyze the obtained data, the quantitative method was most appropriate (Muijs, 2004).

Research Design

I selected a non-experimental descriptive design through which I statistically analyzed the data collected, examined, and described the effects of the demographic factors of race, age, gender, job tenure, job position, or level of education of a bank's employee on job satisfaction post-merger. In a similar study, Brown, Maples, Nabirye, and Pryor (2011) used questionnaires to obtain data and examined the occupational stress, job satisfaction, and job performance of hospital nurses. The descriptive design is appropriate and effective for collecting quantitative data (Daly, Hall, & Madigan, 2010). This design enabled the use of Abridged Job in General (AJIG) questionnaires to generalize from a sample of the population of bank employees.

The validity and reliability of the questions that make up the content of the questionnaire have been determined in a similar dissertation research study conducted by Shelly Baker at Northcentral University (Baker, 2009). Baker used both the Abridged Job Descriptive Index (AJDI) and AJIG instruments to examine the bank's employees' job satisfaction after the M&A. In the current study, I used the AJIG assessment only, because I examined only the job satisfaction of bank employees and did not need the AJDI. The AJDI is appropriate for measuring the job satisfaction levels of different facets of a job, and that is outside the scope of the current study. I obtained approval to use the AJIG questionnaire from JDI office of Bowling Green State University, the copyright owner of the AJIG questionnaire (see Appendix D).

POPULATION AND SAMPLING

The population required for this study was drawn from the employee pool of Sunshine Bank (pseudonym). The bank has employees across the United States but, this quantitative research study was focused on employees in Bucks, Delaware, Montgomery, and Philadelphia counties of Pennsylvania. I selected the participants through purposeful sampling. Purposeful sampling method is most appropriate when participants who meet known standards or conditions are required for a study (Krishnaswamy & Satyaprasad, 2010). The participants were the bank employees who work for Sunshine Bank, in Pennsylvania, and experienced M&A between 2006 and 2009. I used purposeful sampling to ensure that I selected the bank employees with the required criteria.

Using G*Power 3.1.7 software (Buchner, Erdfelder, Faul, & Lang, 2009), I performed an initial a priori power-analysis to determine the sample size necessary for the full six-way ANOVA (Fixed effects, special, main effects and interactions). I used the numerator $df = 2$ and number of groups = 96, with an effect size of 0.35 (f) and a power of 0.80, at alpha level of 0.05. The result of the power analysis was $N = 107$. This result indicated that a sample size of 107 respondents was needed for the full ANOVA model with the minimum number of levels per variable; gender (2 levels), age (2 levels), race (3 levels), education (2 levels), job level (2 levels), and tenure (2 levels). A smaller effect size of 0.25 (f) with the same parameters indicated that 162 respondents were needed. The response rate for this study was 49.3%, based on 217 respondents obtained from a population of 440 employees.

Sunshine Bank was the best candidate for this study for several reasons. The bank is a national bank, and among the largest banks regarding assets in the United States. Sunshine Bank has also undergone more than two M&A since 2006 and has an adequate number of employees who have experienced M&A to address the purpose of the study. I required in the questionnaire that only the employees who were employed by the bank before or during any of the mergers should complete the survey. This helped me to increase the chances of reaching employees who experienced the M&A. All levels of employees were encouraged to participate, from tellers to the CEO.

ETHICAL RESEARCH

I included the informed consent form (see Appendix G) in the linked document e-mailed to participants in such a manner that no participant was able to access the survey without first reading the content of informed consent form. I advised every participant through the informed consent form that he or she had the option to withdraw from participating as long as he or she has not sent the completed survey to me. Once the completed survey was sent, the individual could no longer opt out because I was unable to determine which participant owned which response because of the anonymous nature of the survey. Any participant could withdraw by not e-mailing back the completed survey or by deleting the e-mail received from me. No incentive was provided to the participants. The identities of the participants were not exposed. The questionnaire was framed to avoid any question that may reveal the identity of any participant. Real names or identities that could be traced to individuals or institution, unless approved by the individual or institution will be stored in a flash disk and secured in a locked container for 5 years. After 5 years have elapsed, I will destroy the flash disk.

DATA COLLECTION

Instruments

I used the AJIG questionnaire and demographic questions (see Appendix A) to obtain the data necessary to examine if any relationship exists between the race, gender, age, job tenure, job position, or level of education of a bank's employee and his or her job satisfaction post-merger. AJDI method is a cognitive-based tool or structure used in scoring job satisfaction (Borujeni, Chiappa, Jafari, & Khalilzadeh, 2013). The AJIG scoring model (see Appendix

H) was used to score the result of the survey. I sent e-mails to the participants with a link to the survey for the participants to complete. The participants completed the survey by clicking on the e-mailed link. The raw data are in my possession and is available upon request. Given that the purpose of this study was not to address cause and effect, internal validity was not a concern for the study. No revision was made to the standardized research instrument. I used statistical analysis of variance (ANOVA) at the significance level of .05 to examine the data (Decock, et al., 2010).

I obtained permission to use AJIG from JDI's office at Bowling Green State University, Bowling Green, Ohio, United States (see Appendix D). Other researchers have used the AJIG instrument, augmented with demographic questions. The instrument is known to be reliable and easy to administer (Baker, 2009). Baker (2009) used JDI assessments and demographic questions to examine banks' employees' job satisfaction after an M&A. The use of the JDI and demographic questionnaire as research tools was further validated in Abrahamson and Bormann (2014) in which Abrahamson and Bormann used the AJDI and demographic questionnaire to conduct a research examining the relationship and influence of nurse managers on the job satisfaction levels of staff nurses.

Data Collection Technique

SurveyMonkey®, an online database, was used to collect data and administer the survey (Baker, 2009). To contact and encourage the participants to complete the survey, I called each branch in the stated locations and obtained the e-mail address of the manager at each location. I sent an e-mail to the branch managers and managers of other lines of businesses surveyed (see Appendix B). I requested for managers to complete the survey (see Appendix A) by clicking on the link and forward the e-mails to the rest of the employees to complete the survey within 14 calendar days. Follow-up e-mails were not necessary because the required number of responses were received within 7 days (see Appendix C). Carr, Sanders, and Simmons (2011) sent e-mail invitations to the participants in their online survey (SurveyMonkey®) study of the attitudes and use of biomedical surgical specimen cut-up in the UK. Pilot study was not necessary and was not conducted for the current study.

Data Organization Techniques

SurveyMonkey®, an online database, tracked data and kept records of responses (Baker, 2009; Carr, Sanders, & Simmons, 2011). The electronic data administrator has a secure database for the collection, security, and protection of the data obtained. I downloaded the data from SurveyMonkey® into an Excel spreadsheet and SPSS software. Raw data are kept in locked container and will be destroyed after five years. SurveyMonkey® provides a description of its security measures at http://www.surveymonkey/MonkeyPrivacy.aspx

DATA ANALYSIS TECHNIQUE

The online data administrator, SurveyMonkey®, documented the responses and gave the option to export the data into Microsoft Excel spreadsheet form. I chose SurveyMonkey® for this research because of the successful use of SurveyMonkey® in the past similar research (Baker, 2009). Baker (2009) examined the banks' employees' job satisfaction after the M&A. Baker used Abridged Job Descriptive Index (AJDI) and Abridged Job in General assessments through SurveyMonkey® data collection process to collect and analyze data. Borujeni, Chiappa, Jafari, and Khalilzadeh (2013) used survey and AJDI assessments in their study of job satisfaction levels in hospital firms.

In the study of job satisfaction and turnover intent of primary healthcare nurses in rural South Africa, Decock et al. (2010) used statistical analysis of variance (ANOVA) to calculate job satisfaction. I analyzed the data collected through SurveyMonkey® using the SPSS ANOVA tests, in which the response variable, job satisfaction, was tested for the effects of factors of job tenure, age, race, gender, educational level, and job level. SPSS release 20.0 software allows many data sets to be easily loaded into it and simplifies the analysis of complex data (Herrington & Starkweather, 2014). Dylla et al.

(2014) used SPSS software in their study of the promotion of physical therapist's use of research evidence to inform clinical practice. SPSS can be used for statistical analysis, data management, and documentation (Green & Salkind, 2010; Herrington & Starkweather, 2014). The content of the SPSS release 20.0.0 includes descriptive and bivariate statistics, linear regression, factor analysis, discriminant, and cluster analysis, which provide for effective analysis of research findings. Though the content of SPSS release 20.0.0 includes the mentioned statistical measures capability, I examined only the statistical measures necessary to address the research hypotheses.

I conducted a 6-way ANOVA to examine the main research question, however, because of small cell sizes (< 2) in many of the cells, many of the 3-way interactions and the 4-, 5-, and 6-way interactions would not calculate in SPSS. To increase the cell sizes in for interactions, I collapsed the levels of variables to two levels for five variables (gender was already 2 levels). I collapsed levels or groups to achieve as close to 50% of the sample in each group, as well as making sure the groups made logical conceptual sense. Age was re-coded as under 36 versus 36 and over. Race was collapsed to White/Non-Hispanic, Black and Hispanic/Other. Education was re-coded as high school/GED/Associates degree versus bachelor's degree/master's degree or more. Tenure was collapsed into less than 6 years versus 6 or more years. Job level was re-coded as semiskilled/professionals versus local and regional supervisors and managers.

Collapsing levels of the categorical independent variables together to reduce the number of categories to only two levels as described above created an increase in the sample size in the cells. However, this did not enable the calculating of the four, five, and six-way interactions. Levene's test was violated indicating a violation of the homogeneity of variance assumption, $F(34, 174) = 1.78$, $p = .009$. No significant main effects or 2-factor interactions were found in the 6-way model. Because of the small cell sizes and lack of significance in the six-way interaction, I conducted a series of one-way Analyses of Variance (ANOVAs) to examine the main effects of the variables of interest with the original levels, gender, age, race, education level, job level, and tenure on job satisfaction as measured with the JIG scale. However, to account for the increased likelihood of a Type I error that accompanies a series of hypothesis tests, I used a Bonferroni correction of the alpha level. The Bonferroni correction formula is the original alpha level divided by the number of times the hypothesis is tested. For the current project, this computes to .05/6, or alpha equal to .008.

I used the JIG sum score, which measures job satisfaction, as the primary dependent variable for this research (see Table 2). On average, participants reported a JIG sum score of 42.62 (SD = 8.17) with a minimum of 23 and a maximum of 54. Through the results of the data analysis, an attempt was made to answer the principal research question regarding if bank leaders could develop strategies to stop the exit of top performing employees after the M&A, by examining if any difference exists in the employees' satisfaction levels after the M&A based on job tenure, job title or position, race, gender, age, or level of education. If any strategy could be developed, which could help to address the issue raised by the theoretical framework (Social Identity Theory) of this study, to minimize or eliminate the exit of employees after an M&A. The output from the SPSS programs' one-way ANOVA analyses of the participants' response data obtained using Abridged Job in General (AJIG) assessments and demographic questionnaires demonstrated statistically significant effects at the .05 significance level for the variables job tenure, job title, age, level of education and job satisfaction. No evidence of any relationship was determined between race, gender and job satisfaction. Based on this study, strategies developed based on job tenure, job title, age, and level of education of employees may help to improve satisfaction which affects the exit of employees (the social identity issue of this study) after an M&A (Baker, 2009).

RELIABILITY AND VALIDITY

Reliability

Baker (2009) used the AJIG questionnaire and demographic survey questions in conducting similar research. I collected data through SurveyMonkey® (Baker, 2009). SurveyMonkey® provides a description of its security measures at http://www.surveymonkey/ MonkeyPrivacy.aspx. Krochalk and Snarr (1996) used the JDI and the survey instruments to assess the relationship between the job satisfaction level of the faculty members of a nursing institution and the organizational characteristics of the institution and the nursing program. Past research indicated the Cronbach's alpha estimates of inter-item reliability for the alpha co-efficient for AJIG to be .92 (Beebe, Blaylock, & Sweetser, 2009).

Validity

The use of the ANOVA model was conducted in a prior similar study (Baker, 2009). ANOVA models have several assumptions. The dependent variable must be continuous, normally distributed, and no outliers should be present. The data from different observations should be independent and the variances should be the same throughout the data (homoscedastic; Ha & Ha, 2011). While the assumption of independence was met, there was a violation of the assumption for similar variances in the interaction ANOVA. Also, ANOVA analysis requires all levels of the independent variables should have equal or similar sample sizes (Ha & Ha, 2011). Decock et al. (2010) used the statistical ANOVA in their study of the job satisfaction and turnover intent of primary healthcare nurses in rural South Africa. Because of the small cell sizes in some of the interaction groups, I also conducted separate one-way ANOVAs because not all six variables of interest could be placed in the model at the same time. I conducted Pearson's chi-square tests of independence between independent variables (i.e., gender, age, race, education level, job level, and tenure) to determine if there was multi-collinearity among the independent variables that could affect the primary ANOVA model. I also developed descriptive statistics for the dependent variable (i.e., job satisfaction) to assess the distribution of the variable for parametric analysis, and to identify potential outliers. The dependent variable was continuous, and normally distributed. There were no issues of multi-collinearity found, and no outliers were found on the continuous variables.

Given that the purpose of this study was not to address cause and effect, internal validity was not a concern for the study. No evidence exists that the participants in this study were truthful or not. The personal biases of the participants could have affected their responses. I asked the participants to refrain from allowing personal biases to affect the responses, but no evidence exists that the participants complied or not.

External threats occur when inferences are drawn from outside the boundaries of the population studied (Creswell, 2013). The experiences of the employees were from one major bank in Pennsylvania and may not reflect the experiences of employees from banks in other states. The population studied was from one bank with employees in Bucks, Delaware, Montgomery, and Philadelphia counties of Pennsylvania. The experience or response of the bank's employees in other areas of Pennsylvania and other states may be different. The experiences of bank employees from other banks who experienced M&A could be different.

Other stressors such as goal emphasis, role stress, work ethic, autonomy, and job challenge, which have been identified as important factors of job satisfaction (Chen, Lien, & Lin, 2011), were not included in this study. Literature review revealed that findings from past relative studies showed evidence of external validity within the respective industries (Krochalk & Snarr, 1996). The findings of this study should be interpreted cautiously because of the differences in the experiences and personal perceptions of bank employees who experienced M&A in different banks and locations.

TRANSITION AND SUMMARY

The objective of Section 2 was to provide the background and describe steps I used to design, develop, and conduct the research. I used the results of the research to examine whether demographic factors of job tenure, race, age, gender, level of education, or job level affected participants' job satisfaction. Follow-up e-mails were not necessary because I received required number of responses within seven days. This was a quantitative descriptive study using the AJIG questionnaire and demographic survey questions for collecting data. I collected and tabulated the data using MS Excel and standard summary statistics such as means, standard deviations, and frequencies through SurveyMonkey®. I did additional analysis using SPSS 20.0 ANOVA software to test for the significance of the effects of the employees' demographic variables at .05 level of statistical significance.

Baker (2009) and Krochalk and Snarr (1996) demonstrated the validity and reliability of the AJIG. Krochalk and Snarr used JDI assessments to examine the relationship between the job satisfaction of the faculty members in a nursing institution and the organizational characteristics of the institution and the nursing program. Baker examined the job satisfaction levels of bank employees after an M&A, using the JDI and AJIG assessment tools. Findings from this study are detailed in Section 3.

CHAPTER 3

Application to Professional Practice and Implications for Change

The purpose of this quantitative research study was to examine factors that influence the exit of top-performing employees, including leaders from the banks after the M&A from the perspectives of job tenure, job title, race, age, gender, or level of education of the bank employees. The research question was: What strategies could help bank leaders to forestall the exit of top-performing bank employees, including leaders from the banks after the M&A? I examined the effect of job tenure, job level, race, age, gender, and level of education of bank employees on job satisfaction after the M&A to determine if the demographic factors had any effect on the job satisfaction levels of the bank employees who experienced M&A, and whether the level of job satisfaction affected the employees' decision to stay or leave the bank after the M&A.

OVERVIEW OF STUDY

Bank employees, especially top performers, tend to leave after the M&A (Baker, 2009). The exit of valuable employees poses major business challenges to industry leaders. In this study, I examined factors that influence the exit of top-performing employees, including leaders from the banks after the M&A from the perspectives of job tenure, job title, race, age, gender, or level of education of the bank employees. The research question was designed to examine what strategies could help bank leaders to forestall the exit of top-performing bank employees, including leaders from the banks after the M&A.

I examined the following hypotheses:

$H1_0$: There is no effect of job tenure on job satisfaction for bank employees who have experienced M&A.

$H1_a$: There is an effect of job tenure on job satisfaction for bank employees who have experienced M&A.

$H2_0$: There is no effect of race on job satisfaction for bank employees who have experienced M&A.

$H2_a$: There is an effect of race on job satisfaction for bank employees who have experienced M&A.

$H3_0$: There is no effect of age on job satisfaction for bank employees who have experienced M&A.

$H3_a$: There is an effect of age on job satisfaction for bank employees who have experienced M&A.

$H4_0$: There is no effect of gender on job satisfaction for bank employees who have experienced M&A.

$H4_a$: There is an effect of gender on job satisfaction for bank employees who have experienced M&A.

$H5_0$: There is no effect of level of education on job satisfaction for bank employees who have experienced M&A.

$H5_a$: There is an effect of level of education on job satisfaction for bank employees who have experienced M&A.

$H6_0$: There is no effect of job level or position on job satisfaction for bank employees who have experienced M&A.

$H6_a$: There is an effect of job level or position on job satisfaction of bank employees who have experienced M&A.

The results showed the following:

1. A significant relationship existed between age and job satisfaction after the M&A.
2. A significant relationship existed between the level of education and job satisfaction after the M&A.
3. No statistically significant relationship existed between gender and job satisfaction after the M&A.
4. A significant relationship existed between job positions and job satisfaction after the M&A.

5. No statistically significant relationship existed between race and job satisfaction after the M&A.
6. A significant relationship existed between job tenure and job satisfaction after the M&A.

PRESENTATION OF THE FINDINGS

The purpose of this quantitative research study was to examine factors that influence the exit of top-performing employees, including leaders from the banks after the M&A. I examined the job satisfaction of bank employees after the M&A from the perspectives of the employees' job tenure, job level, race, age, gender, and level of education to determine if the demographic factors had any effect on the job satisfaction levels of the bank employees who experienced M&A, and whether the level of job satisfaction affected the employees' decision to stay or leave the bank after the M&A. To examine this research question, preliminary analyses, including Pearson's chi-square tests of independence were conducted to examine the relationships between independent variables (i.e., gender, age, race, education level, job level, and tenure) to determine if there was multi-collinearity among the independent variables that could affect the primary ANOVA model. I also presented descriptive statistics for the dependent variable (i.e., job satisfaction) to assess the distribution of the variable for parametric analysis, and to identify any outliers. The dependent variable must be continuous, normally distributed, and no outliers should be present. Because of the small cell sizes in some of the interaction groups, I also conducted separate one-way ANOVAs with Bonferoni correction because the six variables of interest could not be placed in the model at the same time.

Preliminary Analysis

Frequencies and percentages for categorical independent variables are displayed in Table 2. Out of 217 total respondents, two individuals declined to report their gender and age. In the sample, there were slightly more men participants (54.4%) than there were women participants (45.6%). Although the majority of respondents were under 25 years of age (30.2%), a considerable number of respondents were from 25 to 35 years old (13.5%), 36 to 45 years old (18.6%), 46 to 55 years old (27.0%), and over 55 years old (10.7%). Regarding participants' races, most respondents were either Black (37.8%) or White (31.3%), but the rest of the participants were Hispanic (15.2%) or Other (15.7%). Regarding participants' education level, about one-third of respondents reported earning high school diplomas or GEDs as their highest education level (33.6%). Another one-third of respondents reported bachelor's degrees as the highest level of education (32.7%). About 23.5% of respondents reported obtaining associate's degrees, but 10.1% of respondents reported completing master's degrees or higher. Regarding participants' job levels, the largest proportion of individuals reported being local supervisors or managers (31.8%), followed by semiskilled workers (24.0%), professional workers (22.6%), and regional supervisors or managers (21.7%). When it came to number of years with an organization (tenure), slightly more than one-third of respondents reported working for their organization for 10 years or more (34.1%), whereas about one-fourth of respondents reported employment with their organization for less than 2 years (24.4%). Approximately one-fourth of respondents reported employment with their organization for 2 to 6 years (24.0%), and 17.5% of respondents reported working for their organization for 6 to 10 years.

Table 2

Frequencies and Percentages for Categorical Independent Variables

	n	%
Gender		
Female	98	45.6
Male	117	54.4
Age		
Under 25 years	65	30.2
25 to 35 years	29	13.5

36 to 45 years	40	18.6
46 to 55 years	58	27.0
Over 55 years	23	10.7
Race		
White	68	31.3
Black	82	37.8
Hispanic	33	15.2
Other	34	15.7
Education level		
High school/GED	73	33.6
Associate's degree	51	23.5
Bachelor's degree	71	32.7
Master's degree or higher	22	10.1
Job level		
Semiskilled	52	24.0
Professional	49	22.6
Local supervisor/manager	69	31.8
Regional supervisor/manager	47	21.7
Years with organization		
Less than 2 years	53	24.4
2 to 6 years	52	24.0
6 to 10 years	38	17.5
10 years or more	74	34.1

Note. Frequencies not summing to $N = 217$ and percentages not summing to 100 reflect missing data.

To examine bivariate relationships among the independent variables (i.e., gender, age, race, education level, job level, and tenure), Pearson's chi-square analyses were conducted. Tables 3 through Table 8 show the results of these analyses, including frequencies, percentages, and significance of relationships between variables. The findings indicate several interesting relationships among the independent variables. As shown in Table 3, a significant relationship existed between age and gender, χ^2 (4) = 12.86, p = .012, Cramer's V = .246. Specifically, participants who were 25 years and younger presented more proportion of women (40.2%) than men (21.6%). Additionally participants who were 46 to 55 years old, presented more proportion of men (33.6%) than women (18.6%). There was also a significant relationship between education level and gender, χ^2 (3) = 16.64, p = .001, Cramer's V = .278 (see Table 3). Specifically, a more proportion of women held high school diplomas or GEDs (41.8%) than did men (26.5%). Also, more proportion of men reported having master's degrees or higher (17.1%) than did women (2.0%). Gender was also found to have a significant association with job level, χ^2 (3) = 23.60, p < .001, Cramer's V = .331 (see Table 3). Among participants who reported being a local supervisor or manager, more proportion was female (38.8%) than were male (25.6%), whereas among participants who were regional supervisors or managers, more proportion was male (34.2%) than were female (7.1%).

Table 3

Frequencies and Percentages for Age, Race, Education Level, Job Level, and Years with Organization by Gender

| | Gender | | | | | |
| | Female | | Male | | | |
	n	%	n	%	χ^2	p
Age					12.86	.012
Under 25 years	39	40.2	25	21.6		
25 to 35 years	14	14.4	15	12.9		
36 to 45 years	19	19.6	21	18.1		
46 to 55 years	18	18.6	39	33.6		
Over 55 years	7	7.2	16	13.8		

	Female		Male			
	n	%	n	%	χ^2	p
Race					5.60	.133
White	28	28.6	39	33.3		
Black	43	43.9	38	32.5		
Hispanic	10	10.2	23	19.7		
Other	17	17.3	17	14.5		
Education level					16.64	.001
High school/GED	41	41.8	31	26.5		
Associate's degree	26	26.5	25	21.4		
Bachelor's degree	29	29.6	41	35.0		
Master's degree or higher	2	2.0	20	17.1		
Job level					23.60	< .001
Semiskilled	29	29.6	22	18.8		
Professional	24	24.5	25	21.4		
Local supervisor/manager	38	38.8	30	25.6		
Regional supervisor/manager	7	7.1	40	34.2		
Years with organization					7.28	.064
Less than 2 years	30	30.6	22	18.8		
2 to 6 years	26	26.5	26	22.2		
6 to 10 years		17.3	21	17.9		
10 years or more	25	25.5	48	41.0		

Table 4 displays frequencies and percentages of gender, race, education level, job level, and tenure by age. A Pearson's chi-square test revealed a significant relationship between education level and age, χ^2 (12) = 109.34, $p < .001$, Cramer's $V = .412$. Among respondents who had high school diplomas or GEDs, more proportion were under 25 years old (76.9%) compared to respondents who were 25 to 35 years old (31.0%), 36 to 45 years old (7.5%), 46 to 55 years old (5.2%), and over 55 years old (26.1%). Additionally, more proportion of participants who had high school diplomas or GEDs were between 25 to 35 years old than were participants who were 46 to 55 years old. A smaller proportion of participants who had bachelor's degrees were under 25 years old (3.1%) than were participants who were 25 to 35 years old (31.0%), 36 to 45 years old (55.0%), 46 to 55 years old (51.7%), and over 55 years old (34.8%). A smaller proportion of participants with master's degrees were under 25 years old (0.0%) than were participants who were 46 to 55 years old (22.4%) and over 55 years old (17.4%).

There was significant relationship between job level and age, χ^2 (12) = 246.62, p < .001, Cramer's V = .618. More proportion of semiskilled respondents were under 25 years old (75.4%) than were semiskilled respondents who were 25 to 35 years old (0.0%), 36 to 45 years old (0.0%), 46 to 55 years of age (0.0%), and over 55 years old (4.3%). More proportion of professional respondents were from 25 to 35 years old (75.9%) than were professional respondents who were under 25 years old (24.6%), 36 to 45 years old (15.0%), 46 to 55 years old (6.9%), and over 55 years old (4.3%). A smaller proportion of local supervisors or managers were under 25 years old (0.0%) than were local supervisors or managers who were 25 to 35 years old (20.7%), 36 to 45 years old (70.0%), 46 to 55 years old (43.1%), and over 55 years old (43.5%). Additionally, more proportion of local supervisors or managers were from 36 to 45 years old than were local supervisors or managers who were 25 to 35 years old. For example, more proportion of regional supervisors or managers were from 46 to 55 years old (50.0%) and over 55 years old (47.8%) than were regional supervisors or managers who were from 36 to 45 years old (15.0%), 25 to 35 years old (3.4%), and under 25 years old (0.0%). Furthermore, more proportion of regional supervisors or managers were from 36 to 45 years old than were regional supervisors or managers who were under 25 years old.

A significant relationship was found between tenure and age, χ^2 (12) = 268.22, p < .001, Cramer's V = .645 (see Table 4). Of participants who had less than 2 years tenure, a more proportion were less than 25 years of age (75.4%) than were participants who were 25 to 35 years old (3.4%), 36 to 45 years old (2.5%), 46 to 55 years old (0.0%), and over 55 years old (4.3%). Of participants who had 2 to 6 years tenure, more were from 25 to 35 years old (72.4%) than were participants who were less than 25 years old (24.6%), 36 to 45 years old (32.5%), 46 to 55 years old (1.7%), and over 55 years old (0.0%). For participants who had 6 to 10 years tenure, more proportion were from 36 to 45 years (45.0%) than were participants who were under 25 years old (0.0%) and participants over 55 years old (4.3%). For participants who had at least 10 years tenure, more were from 46 to 55 years old (77.6%) and over 55 years old (91.3%) than were participants who were less than 25 years old (0.0%), 25 to 35 years old (0.0%), and 36 to 45 years old (20.0%). More proportion of respondents who had at least 10 years tenure were 36 to 45 years old than were participants who were under 25 years.

Table 5 displays the frequencies and percentages for gender, age, education level, job level, and tenure by race. A Pearson's chi-square test revealed a significant relationship between job level and race, χ^2 (9) = 22.16, p = .008, Cramer's V = .184. More regional supervisors or managers were White (33.8%) than were Other (8.8%). A significance existed between tenure and race, χ^2 (9) = 19.98, p = .018, Cramer's V = .175 (see Table 5). Fewer respondents with less than 2 years tenure were White (14.7%) than Other (44.1%). Among respondents who were with their organization for 10 years or more, more proportion was White (42.6%) and Black (41.5%) than Hispanic (15.2%).

Table 4

Frequencies and Percentages for Gender, Race, Education Level, Job Level, and Years with Organization by Age

	Age									
	Under 25 years		25 to 35 years		36 to 45 years		46 to 55 years		Over 55 years	
	n	%	n	%	n	%	n	%	n	%
Gender										
Female	39	60.9	14	48.3	19	47.5	18	31.6	7	30.4
Male	25	39.1	15	51.7	21	52.5	39	68.4	16	69.6
Race										
White	16	24.6	9	31.0	9	22.5	23	39.7	11	47.8
Black	22	33.8	7	24.1	18	45.0	26	44.8	8	34.8
Hispanic	11	16.9	7	24.1	6	15.0	5	8.6	3	13.0
Other	16	24.6	6	20.7	7	17.5	4	6.9	1	4.3
Education level										
High school/GED	50	76.9	9	31.0	3	7.5	3	5.2	6	26.1
Associate's degree	13	20.0	10	34.5	11	27.5	12	20.7	5	21.7
Bachelor's degree	2	3.1	9	31.0	22	55.0	30	51.7	8	34.8
Master's degree or higher	0	.0	1	3.4	4	10.0	13	22.4	4	17.4

	Under 25 years		25 to 35 years		Age 36 to 45 years		46 to 55 years		Over 55 years	
	n	%	n	%	n	%	n	%	n	%
Job level										
Semiskilled	49	75.4	0	.0	0	.0	0	.0	1	4.3
Professional	16	24.6	22	75.9	6	15.0	4	6.9	1	4.3
Local supervisor/manager	0	.0	6	20.7	28	70.0	25	43.1	10	43.5
Regional supervisor/manager	0	.0	1	3.4	6	15.0	29	50.0	11	47.8
Years with organization										
Less than 2 years	49	75.4	1	3.4	1	2.5	0	.0	1	4.3
2 to 6 years	16	24.6	21	72.4	13	32.5	1	1.7	0	.0
6 to 10 years	0	.0	7	24.1	18	45.0	12	20.7	1	4.3
10 years or more	0	.0	0	.0	8	20.0	45	77.6	21	91.3

Note: A significant relationship exists between age and gender, $\chi^2 (4) = 12.86$, $p = .012$, Cramer's $V = .246$. No relationship exists between age and race, $\chi^2 (12) = 20.18$, $p = .064$, Cramer's $V = .177$. A significant relationship exists between age and education level, $\chi^2 (12) = 109.34$, $p < .001$, Cramer's $V = .412$. A significant relationship exists between age and job level, $\chi^2 (12) = 246.62$, $p < .001$, Cramer's $V = .618$. A significant relationship exists between age and years with organization (tenure), $\chi^2 (12) = 268.22$, $p < .001$, Cramer's $V = .645$.

Table 5
Frequencies and Percentages for Gender, Age, Education Level, Job Level, and Years with Organization by Race

	Race							
	White		Black		Hispanic		Other	
	n	%	n	%	n	%	n	%
Gender								
Female	28	41.8	43	53.1	10	30.3	17	50.0
Male	39	58.2	38	46.9	23	69.7	17	50.0
Age								
Under 25 years	16	23.5	22	27.2	11	34.4	16	47.1
25 to 35 years	9	13.2	7	8.6	7	21.9	6	17.6
36 to 45 years	9	13.2	18	22.2	6	18.8	7	20.6
46 to 55 years	23	33.8	26	32.1	5	15.6	4	11.8
Over 55 years	11	16.2	8	9.9	3	9.4	1	2.9
Education level								
High school/GED	21	30.9	26	31.7	11	33.3	15	44.1
Associate's degree	11	16.2	20	24.4	10	30.3	10	29.4
Bachelor's degree	27	39.7	26	31.7	10	30.3	8	23.5
Master's degree or higher	9	13.2	10	12.2	2	6.1	1	2.9

| | Race | | | | | | | |
| | White | | Black | | Hispanic | | Other | |
	n	%	n	%	n	%	n	%
Job level								
Semiskilled	13	19.1	15	18.3	10	30.3	14	41.2
Professional	13	19.1	17	20.7	11	33.3	8	23.5
Local supervisor/manager	19	27.9	35	42.7	6	18.2	9	26.5
Regional supervisor/manager	23	33.8	15	18.3	6	18.2	3	8.8
Years with organization								
Less than 2 years	10	14.7	18	22.0	10	30.3	15	44.1
2 to 6 years	17	25.0	16	19.5	11	33.3	8	23.5
6 to 10 years	12	17.6	14	17.1	7	21.2	5	14.7
10 years or more	29	42.6	34	41.5	5	15.2	6	17.6

Note: No relationship exists between race and gender, $\chi^2 (3) = 5.60$, $p = .133$, Cramer's $V = .161$. No relationship exists between race and age, $\chi^2 (12) = 20.18$, $p = .064$, Cramer's $V = .177$. No relationship exists between race and education level, $\chi^2 (9) = 9.33$, $p = .407$, Cramer's $V = .120$. A significant relationship exists between race and job level, $\chi^2 (9) = 22.16$, $p = .008$, Cramer's $V = .184$. A significant relationship exists between race and years with organization (tenure), $\chi^2 (9) = 19.98$, $p = .018$, Cramer's $V = .175$.

Table 6 displays the frequencies and percentages for gender, age, race, job level, and tenure by education level. A Pearson's chi-square test revealed a significance between job level and education level, χ^2 (9) = 213.80, $p < .001$, Cramer's $V = .573$. More semiskilled respondents had high school diplomas or GEDs (67.1%) than did semiskilled respondents with Associate's degrees (5.9%), bachelor's degrees (0.0%), or master's degrees or higher (0.0%). More professional respondents had Associate's degrees (51.0%) than did professionals with high school diplomas or GEDs (23.3%), bachelor's degrees (8.5%), or master's degrees or higher (0.0%). Of local supervisors or managers, more had bachelor's degrees (50.7%) than did local supervisors or managers with high school diplomas or GEDs (9.6%), or master's degrees or higher (18.2%). More local supervisors or managers had associate's degrees (43.1%) than did local supervisors or managers with high school diplomas or GEDs. Of regional supervisors or managers, more had master's degrees or higher (81.8%) than did regional supervisors or managers with bachelor's degrees (40.8%), and more had bachelor's degrees than they had associate's degrees (0.0%) or high school diplomas or GEDs (0.0%).

A significant relationship was also found between tenure and education level, χ^2 (9) = 114.17 $p < .001$, Cramer's $V = .419$ (see Table 6). For participants with less than 2 years tenure, more had high school diplomas or GEDs (60.3%) than had associate's degrees (13.7%), bachelor's degrees (2.8%), or master's degrees or higher (0.0%). For participants with 2 to 6 years tenure, more had associate's degrees (43.1%) than had bachelor's degrees (14.1%) or master's degrees or higher (9.1%). For participants with 6 to 10 years tenure, more had bachelor's degrees (31.0%) or master's degrees or higher (22.7%) than had high school diplomas or GEDs (4.1%). For participants with at least 10 years tenure, more had bachelor's degrees (52.1%) or master's degrees or higher (68.2%) than had associate's degrees (27.5%) or high school diplomas or GEDs (11.0%).

Table 7 shows frequencies and percentages for gender, age, race, education level, and tenure by job level. A Pearson's chi-square test revealed a significant relationship between respondents' tenure and job level, χ^2 (9) = 252.82, $p < .001$, Cramer's $V = .623$. Of participants with less than 2 years tenure, more were semiskilled (86.5%) than were professional (14.3%), local supervisors or managers (1.4%), or regional supervisors or managers (0.0%); more participants with less than 2 years tenure were professional than were local or regional supervisors. Of participants with 2 to 6 years tenure, more were professional (71.4%) than were semiskilled (13.5%), local supervisors or managers (11.6%), or regional supervisors or managers (4.3%). The participants who had 6 to 10 years tenure, 34.8% were local supervisors or managers, professionals (8.2%) and semiskilled (0.0%). Of participants with at least 10 years tenure, more were local (52.2%) or regional supervisors (74.5%) than professionals (6.1%) or semiskilled (0.0%) were. Table 8 displays the frequencies and percentages for gender, age, race, educational level, and job level by tenure. The findings in the table are represented in the write-ups for Tables 4–7. This table shows the percentages by tenure level.

Table 6

Frequencies and Percentages for Gender, Age, Race, Job Level, and Years with Organization by Education Level

	High school/GED		Associate's degree		Bachelor's degree		Master's degree or higher	
	n	*%*	*n*	*%*	*n*	*%*	*n*	*%*
Gender								
Female	41	56.9	26	51.0	29	41.4	2	9.1
Male	31	43.1	25	49.0	41	58.6	20	90.9
Age								
Under 25 years	50	70.4	13	25.5	2	2.8	0	.0
25 to 35 years	9	12.7	10	19.6	9	12.7	1	4.5
36 to 45 years	3	4.2	11	21.6	22	31.0	4	18.2
46 to 55 years	3	4.2	12	23.5	30	42.3	13	59.1
Over 55 years	6	8.5	5	9.8	8	11.3	4	18.2
Race								
White	21	28.8	11	21.6	27	38.0	9	40.9
Black	26	35.6	20	39.2	26	36.6	10	45.5
Hispanic	11	15.1	10	19.6	10	14.1	2	9.1

Education level

| | Education level | | | | | | | |
| | High school/GED | | Associate's degree | | Bachelor's degree | | Master's degree or higher | |
	n	%	n	%	n	%	n	%
Other	15	20.5	10	19.6	8	11.3	1	4.5
Job level								
Semiskilled	49	67.1	3	5.9	0	.0	0	.0
Professional	17	23.3	26	51.0	6	8.5	0	.0
Local supervisor/manager	7	9.6	22	43.1	36	50.7	4	18.2
Regional supervisor/manager	0	.0	0	.0	29	40.8	18	81.8
Years with organization								
Less than 2 years	44	60.3	7	13.7	2	2.8	0	.0
2 to 6 years	18	24.7	22	43.1	10	14.1	2	9.1
6 to 10 years	3	4.1	8	15.7	22	31.0	5	22.7
10 years or more	8	11.0	14	27.5	37	52.1	15	68.2

Note: A significant relationship exists between education level and gender, $\chi^2(3) = 16.64$, $p < .001$, Cramer's $V = .278$. A significant relationship exists between education level and age, $\chi^2(12) = 109.34$, $p < .001$, Cramer's $V = .412$. No relationship exists between education level and race, $\chi^2(9) = 9.33$, $p = .407$, Cramer's $V = .120$. A significant relationship exists between education level and job level, $\chi^2(9) = 213.80$, $p < .001$, Cramer's $V = .573$. A significant relationship exists between education level and years with organization (tenure), $\chi^2(9) = 114.17$ $p < .001$, Cramer's $V = .419$.

Table 7
Frequencies and Percentages for Gender, Age, Race, Education Level, and Years with Organization by Job Level

	Job level							
	Semiskilled		Professional		Local supervisor/ manager		Regional supervisor/ manager	
	n	%	n	%	n	%	n	%
Gender								
Female	29	56.9	24	49.0	38	55.9	7	14.9
Male	22	43.1	25	51.0	30	44.1	40	85.1
Age								
Under 25 years	49	98.0	16	32.7	0	.0	0	.0
25 to 35 years	0	.0	22	44.9	6	8.7	1	2.1
36 to 45 years	0	.0	6	12.2	28	40.6	6	12.8
46 to 55 years	0	.0	4	8.2	25	36.2	29	61.7
Over 55 years	1	2.0	1	2.0	10	14.5	11	23.4
Race								
White	13	25.0	13	26.5	19	27.5	23	48.9
Black	15	28.8	17	34.7	35	50.7	15	31.9
Hispanic	10	19.2	11	22.4	6	8.7	6	12.8
Other	14	26.9	8	16.3	9	13.0	3	6.4

| | Job level | | | | | | | |
| | Semiskilled | | Professional | | Local supervisor/ manager | | Regional supervisor/ manager | |
	n	%	n	%	n	%	n	%
Education level								
High school/GED	49	94.2	17	34.7	7	10.1	0	.0
Associate's degree	3	5.8	26	53.1	22	31.9	0	.0
Bachelor's degree	0	.0	6	12.2	36	52.2	29	61.7
Master's degree or higher	0	.0	0	.0	4	5.8	18	38.3
Years with organization								
Less than 2 years	45	86.5	7	14.3	1	1.4	0	.0
2 to 6 years	7	13.5	35	71.4	8	11.6	2	4.3
6 to 10 years	0	.0	4	8.2	24	34.8	10	21.3
10 years or more	0	.0	3	6.1	36	52.2	35	74.5

Note: A significant relationship exists between job level and gender, $\chi^2 (3) = 23.60, p < .001$, Cramer's $V = .331$. A significant relationship exists between job level and age, $\chi^2 (12) = 246.62, p < .001$, Cramer's $V = .618$. A significant relationship exists between job level and race, $\chi^2 (9) = 22.16, p = .008$, Cramer's $V = .184$. A significant relationship exists between job level and education level, $\chi^2 (9) = 213.80, p < .001$, Cramer's $V = .573$. A significant relationship exists between job level and years with organization (tenure), $\chi^2 (9) = 252.82, p < .001$, Cramer's $V = .623$.

Table 8

Frequencies and Percentages for Gender, Age, Race, Education Level, and Job Level by Years with Organization

| | Years with organization | | | | | | | |
| | Less than 2 years | | 2 to 6 years | | 6 to 10 years | | 10 years or more | |
	n	%	n	%	n	%	n	%
Gender								
Female	30	57.7	26	50.0	17	44.7	25	34.2
Male	22	42.3	26	50.0	21	55.3	48	65.8
Age								
Under 25 years	49	94.2	16	31.4	0	.0	0	.0
25 to 35 years	1	1.9	21	41.2	7	18.4	0	.0
36 to 45 years	1	1.9	13	25.5	18	47.4	8	10.8
46 to 55 years	0	.0	1	2.0	12	31.6	45	60.8
Over 55 years	1	1.9	0	.0	1	2.6	21	28.4
Race								
White	10	18.9	17	32.7	12	31.6	29	39.2
Black	18	34.0	16	30.8	14	36.8	34	45.9
Hispanic	10	18.9	11	21.2	7	18.4	5	6.8
Other	15	28.3	8	15.4	5	13.2	6	8.1

| | Years with organization | | | | | | | |
| | Less than 2 years | | 2 to 6 years | | 6 to 10 years | | 10 years or more | |
	n	%	n	%	n	%	n	%
Education level								
High school/GED	44	83.0	18	34.6	3	7.9	8	10.8
Associate's degree	7	13.2	22	42.3	8	21.1	14	18.9
Bachelor's degree	2	3.8	10	19.2	22	57.9	37	50.0
Master's degree or higher	0	.0	2	3.8	5	13.2	15	20.3
Job level								
Semiskilled	45	84.9	7	13.5	0	.0	0	.0
Professional	7	13.2	35	67.3	4	10.5	3	4.1
Local supervisor/manager	1	1.9	8	15.4	24	63.2	36	48.6
Regional supervisor/ manager	0	.0	2	3.8	10	26.3	35	47.3

Note: No relationship exists between years with organization and gender, $\chi^2 (3) = 7.28$, $p = .064$, Cramer's $V = .184$. A significant relationship exists between years with organization and age, $\chi^2 (12) = 268.22$, $p < .001$, Cramer's $V = .645$. A significant relationship exists between years with organization and race, $\chi^2 (9) = 19.98$, $p = .018$, Cramer's $V = .175$. A significant relationship exists between years with organization and education level, $\chi^2 (9) = 114.17$ $p < .001$, Cramer's $V = .419$. A significant relationship exists between years with organization and job level, $\chi^2 (9) = 252.82$, $p < .001$, Cramer's $V = .623$.

I used the JIG sum score, which measures job satisfaction, as the primary dependent variable (see Table 9). On average, participants reported an overall JIG sum score of 42.62 (*SD* = 8.17) with a minimum of 23 and a maximum of 54.

Table 9

Means and Standard Deviations for JIG Sum Score

	N	*M*	*SD*	Min	Max
JIG Sum Score	213	42.62	8.17	23	54

Primary Analysis

Because of the small cell sizes in the 6-factor interaction model even with using all 2 level variables, I conducted a series of one-way ANOVA to examine the main effects of the variables of interest with the original levels, gender, age, race, education level, job level, and tenure on job satisfaction as measured with the JIG scale. However, to account for the increased likelihood of a Type I error that accompanies a series of hypothesis tests, a Bonferroni correction of the alpha level was performed (Bauer & Graf, 2011; Bauer, Glimm, Graf, & Koenig, 2014). The Bonferroni correction formula is the original alpha level divided by the number of times the hypothesis is tested. For the current project, this computed to .05/6, or alpha equal to .008.

As shown in Table 10, age significantly affected job satisfaction, F (4, 206) = 5.75, $p < .001$. Tukey's HSD post-hoc tests revealed that participants who were 46 to 55 years old ($M = 46.13$, $SD = 7.52$) reported more job satisfaction than did participants who were under 25 years old ($M = 39.91$, $SD = 8.00$) and participants who were 25 to 35 years old ($M = 40.45$, $SD = 7.32$), $p < .05$. Education level also significantly affected job satisfaction, F (3, 209) = 5.52, $p = .001$. Tukey HSD post-hoc tests revealed that participants with high school diplomas or GEDs reported less job satisfaction ($M = 39.60$, $SD = 7.48$) than did participants with Associate's degrees ($M = 43.71$, $SD = 6.32$), Bachelor's degrees ($M = 44.09$, $SD = 8.86$), or

Master's degrees or higher ($M = 45.48$, $SD = 9.48$), $p < .05$. Job level significantly affected job satisfaction, F (3, 209) = 13.30, $p < .001$. Tukey HSD post-hoc tests revealed that regional supervisors and managers reported more job satisfaction ($M = 48.17$, $SD = 5.68$) than did local supervisors or managers ($M = 42.33$, $SD = 8.30$), professionals ($M = 41.71$, $SD = 7.83$), or semiskilled workers ($M = 38.73$, $SD = 7.71$), $p < .05$. Last, tenure significantly affected job satisfaction, F (3, 209) = 6.28, $p < .001$. Tukey HSD post-hoc tests revealed that participants who worked for an organization for less than 2 years reported less job satisfaction ($M = 39.04$, $SD = 7.99$) than did participants who worked for an organization for 6 to 10 years ($M = 45.21$, $SD = 6.64$) or 10 years or more ($M = 44.38$, $SD = 7.97$), $p < .05$. Gender and race did not significantly affect job satisfaction, all *p values* > .150.

Table 10

One-Way ANOVAs for JIG Sum Score by Gender, Age, Race, Education Level, Job Level, and Years with Organization

	n	M	SD	F	p
Gender				.84	.359
Female	97	43.14	7.62		
Male	114	42.11	8.64		
Age				5.75	< .001
Under 25 years	64	39.91	8.00		
25 to 35 years	29	40.45	7.32		
36 to 45 years	39	44.18	8.28		
46 to 55 years	56	46.13	7.52		
Over 55 years	23	42.78	7.33		
Race				1.78	.152
White	67	42.27	7.85		
Black	80	43.98	8.73		

Hispanic	33	42.45	7.53		
Other	33	40.18	7.70		
Education level				5.52	.001
High school/GED	72	39.60	7.48		
Associate's degree	51	43.71	6.32		
Bachelor's degree	69	44.09	8.86		
Master's degree or higher	21	45.48	9.48		
Job level				13.30	< .001
Semiskilled	51	38.73	7.71		
Professional	49	41.71	7.83		
Local supervisor/ manager	66	42.33	8.30		
Regional supervisor/ manager	47	48.17	5.68		
Years with organization				6.28	< .001
Less than 2 years	52	39.04	7.99		
2 to 6 years	52	41.88	8.45		
6 to 10 years	38	45.21	6.64		
10 years or more	71	44.38	7.97		

SUMMARY

In this study, I examined how much bank employees' job satisfaction after a merger and acquisition may be related to gender, age, race, education level, job level, and tenure, to help identify strategy to forestall the exit of top performing employees after an M&A. When examined separately, the variables age, education level, job level, and tenure significantly affected job satisfaction. Specifically, employees from 46 to 55 years of age reported more job satisfaction than did younger employees. Additionally, employees with associate's degrees, bachelor's degrees, or master's degrees or higher reported more job satisfaction than did individuals with high school diplomas or GEDs. Regional supervisors and managers reported more job satisfaction than did employees at any other job level (i.e., local supervisors or managers, professionals, and semiskilled employees). Finally, employees with at least 6 years tenure reported more job satisfaction than did employees with less than 2 years tenure.

The findings supported the following hypotheses: H_{1a} (effect of job tenure), H_{3a} (effect of age), H_{5a} (effect of level of education), H_{6a} (effect of job level). However, the findings failed to support the following hypotheses: H_{2a} (effect of race) and H_{4a} (effect of gender). The results are the same as the results obtained by Baker (2009) regarding the effects of age and job position. Baker's findings differ from the current findings on the effects of job tenure, gender, and level of education. The differing findings present opportunity for future research.

Strategies developed based on job tenure, job title, age, and level of education of employees may help to address the issue raised by the theoretical framework of this study. The review of literature showed that M&A is a valid strategy for enhancing business growth (Assaf, Barros, & Ibiwoye, 2012; Malul, Meydani, & Shoham, 2012; Phillips & Zhdanov, 2013). The review, however, indicated the need for primary issues, such as social identity issues are addressed for an M&A to be successful. The findings of the current study validate this position (as revealed by the literature review). Table 11 shows the similarities and differences between current study and Baker (2009).

Table 11

Similarities and Differences Between Current Study and Baker (2009)

Current Study	Baker's Study at NCU
The current research has only one principal research question and examined: The job satisfaction of bank employees after an M&A based on their job tenure, job level, race, age, gender, and level of education.	Dr. Baker's study involved two research questions and examined: (a) The differences in job satisfaction levels of bank employees who experienced M&A based on their age, gender, job level, job tenure, and level of education. (b) Whether there were differences among job facets of work on present job, supervision, opportunities for promotion, people at work, and present pay for the bank employees who participated in the study.
I used the Abridged Job in General (AJIG) and demographic questionnaires to collect data through surveymonkey.com	Baker used the Abridged Job Descriptive Index (AJDI), Abridged Job in General (AJIG) and demographic questionnaires to collect data through surveymonkey.com
Examination of the differences between different job facets is outside the scope of the current study.	Baker used the AJDI scale to examine any difference between the different job facets for the bank employees.

In the current study, the findings showed that:

- A relationship exists between the age, job tenure, job title, level of education of bank employees, and job satisfaction after the M&A.
- No significant relationship was found between race, gender, and job satisfaction.

Baker found the following:

- That age had an effect on job satisfaction, especially for employees over 40 years of age.
- That gender had no effect.
- That job level had an effect especially among bank employees with higher job levels.
- That job tenure had no effect.
- And that level of education had no effect.

APPLICATIONS TO PROFESSIONAL PRACTICE

Findings from the current study add to the existing literature in helping bank merger administrators to understand some of the demographic factors related to job satisfaction of bank employees after the M&A. Satisfied bank employees do not leave the bank after the M&A, thereby helping to make the M&A successful (Baker, 2009). Results of the current study helped show important factors, such as job tenure, level of education, age, and job position of bank employees. If addressed appropriately, these important factors could positively affect the level of satisfaction of employees. Bank leaders could deploy the available resources to enhance these identified demographic factors to facilitate more mergers that are successful.

The exit of top performers, including leaders, is a problem banks' leaders experience after M&A (Krug, 2009). Good employees leave the merged banks because of dissatisfaction and anxiety over the merger (Baker, 2009; Bellou, 2007; Konstantopoulos et al., 2009; Krug, 2009). If merger administrators enhance the identified factors (job tenure, job level, age, and level of education of employees), those measures could contribute to the increased job satisfaction levels of bank employees. Employees with high job satisfaction and motivated tend to perform better after an M&A (Nadiri & Tanova, 2010). The findings validate the relevance of social identity issues, and bank leaders could benefit from this study by deploying strategies: timely and effective communication and enhanced job satisfaction of employees to diminish or eliminate any social identity issue that may arise after the M&A. Happy employees tend to stay with the bank, and dissatisfied employees may leave after the M&A (do Monte, 2012). This strategy could be accomplished by reviewing bank employees' job tenure, job level, age, and level of education before M&A and applying the obtained information as appropriate throughout the merger process. If the above steps are taken appropriately, bank employees' job performances could improve, more top performing employees may be retained, and more M&A efforts would become successful.

IMPLICATIONS FOR SOCIAL CHANGE

Bank merger administrators could obtain useful information from the results of this study regarding the potential effects of race, age, gender, job tenure, job position, or level of education of bank employees on job satisfaction after the M&A. The administrators should consider the effects of the identified factors as they implement future M&A. Executing M&A in a manner sensitive to the demographic factors could benefit the stakeholders, as the morale and satisfaction of the bank employees will be improved. Under this circumstance, the employees will tend to perform better and produce more for the organization (Austin & Benton, 2010). The financial returns for the shareholders may increase. This may also increase the employee retention rate as satisfied employees choose to stay with the bank (Baker, 2009). The increase in the number of employees retained may help to provide the community with gainfully employed taxpayers who contribute to the economy and may perform civic duties. A successfully executed M&A helps the organization, the community, and shareholders to achieve the goal, and employees do not worry about job security (Hackbarth & Miao, 2012).

RECOMMENDATIONS FOR ACTION

M&A when properly implemented can be a source of capital growth and expanded market reach for banks (Ashton, 2012). However, for any M&A to be successful, the merger administrators must recognize the importance of treating the employees as valuable assets. The bank leaders should ensure that the employees do not perceive the M&A as a threat to their personal or professional growth. If the employees are motivated, not anxious and uncertain about the merger, the employees' reactions to the merger will be positive (Teerikangas, 2010). The acquirer company should demonstrate consistent positive future intentions and the target company should re-enforce a strategic positive response to the merger. The target company should proactively promote the acquisition success and demonstrate the need to be acquired (Teerikangas, 2010).

The M&A could fail if the cultures of the merging organizations are not properly integrated (Schroeder, 2012). The integration process must include (a) trust, (b) communication, (c) teaching transfer, and (d) fairness of treatment. The integration of these primary functions can ensure that the new company moves in a unified direction.

The merger administrators need to be conscious of the job tenure, age, job position, and level of education of the employees as these may affect the job satisfaction of the employees as evidenced in the current study. The effects of these demographic factors could influence the exit of top performing employees at the bank after the M&A. Dissatisfied employees tend to leave the bank after the M&A (Baker, 2009). The leaders should take steps to build a relationship with the employees and protect the relationship that exists among the employees. Protecting and enhancing the relationship among the employees could strengthen the social identities built by the employees over the years of working together (Baker, 2009). Otherwise, employees may choose to leave the bank after the M&A because of job dissatisfaction. Employee turnover affects the social identities of the employees negatively. The leaders can avoid these potential challenges by implementing timely communications, and providing forums for feedbacks from the employees. The results of this study are most relevant to bank leaders and bank merger administrators. The results can be disseminated through publications on the Journals of American Institute of Banking (AIB) and American Bankers Association (ABA).

RECOMMENDATIONS FOR FURTHER STUDY

The current study addressed bank employees who stayed with the bank after the M&A. The employees who are currently employed by the bank completed the demographic and AJIG questionnaires and provided information on how their job tenure, race, age, gender, job position, or level of education affected their job satisfaction after the M&A. For a subsequent study, researchers should consider interviewing former employees who left the bank voluntarily after the M&A. This could provide additional information about why bank employees leave the bank after the M&A, and what role job satisfaction plays in the decision process.

The new information from this study can help bank merger administrators in understanding some of the factors likely to affect the job satisfaction of employees and the employees' decision to leave; this way, the administrators will be able to manage the employee turnovers effectively to increase the likelihood of successful mergers. The effective management of the turnover will help to preserve the social identity built by the employees over the years of working together, creating job satisfaction among employees, and contributing to successful bank mergers.

REFLECTIONS

I assured the participants of anonymity which perhaps enabled them to be candid in their participation. The active participation I received while conducting the research could mean that associates are eager to find a solution to employee turnover commonly seen after the M&A. Associates value the relationships built with each other over the years of working together. The exit of top performing employees after the M&A negatively affects the social identities established by the employees.

I was objective and looked forward to the findings. I examined the effects of demographic factors such as (a) race, (b) age, (c) gender, (d) job tenure, (e) job position, and (f) level of education on job satisfaction. The findings indicated that race and gender are not significant factors to determine the job satisfaction of bank employees after the M&A. The results of the study were insightful for me particularly on race and gender. If the respondents for this study were truthful, the lack of any effect of race or gender on the job satisfaction of the employees could be a reflection of societal growth in race relations and gender equality.

SUMMARY AND STUDY CONCLUSIONS

The job satisfaction of bank employees after the M&A is critical to the success of the M&A. The bank leaders should focus on improved profitability and increased strength in the banking industry, but the leaders must also consider the human element of any merger transaction in the form of the employees acquired in the merger process. The employees should not be seen or treated as only part of costs that could be cut (Adjei-Benin & Sanda, 2011). The employees should be recognized and appreciated for their roles in successful M&A and achievement of the goals of the organization. They should be motivated, informed, and fully integrated into the merger process (Addison & Lloyd, 1999).

Merger administrators should avoid mergers that could create incompatible management cultures and conflicting marketing strategies (Sagner, 2012). The administrators should design a clear plan that will integrate the managerial executives, financial, and control systems of the merging banks to ensure a unified direction. The vision and mission of the new company must be aligned to help optimize strength and achieve synergy (Addison & Lloyd, 1999; Sagner, 2012). The importance of the human resources aspects of the M&A cannot be overemphasized.

To ensure bank employees' job satisfaction, leaders should consider the (a) job tenure, (b) job position, (c) age, and (d) level of education of the employees. If employees are dissatisfied, they may seek an opportunity outside the bank (Krug, 2009). The exit of top talents after the M&A makes it difficult for bank leaders to achieve the goals of the merger. Retention of valuable employees will help to sustain the social identity built by the employees over the years of working together, and increase the job satisfaction levels among the employees. Employees who have high job satisfaction levels perform well and could be the cornerstone for the success of the M&A (Kumar, & Pak, & Rose, 2009).

References

Abdullah, M. M. B., & Islam, R. (2012). Employee motivational factors: A comparison between Malaysia and Sultanate of Oman. *Journal for Global Business Advancement, 5*(4), 285–306. doi:10.1504/JGBA.2012.052390

Abrahamson, K., & Bormann, L. (2014). Do staff nurse perceptions of nurse leadership behaviors influence staff nurse job satisfaction? The case of a hospital applying for Magnet® designation. *The Journal of Nursing Administration, 44*, 219–225. doi:10.1097/NNA.0000000000000053

Addison, R. M., & Lloyd, C. R. (1999). Implementation: The glue of organizational change. *Performance Improvement, 38*(6), 8–11. doi:10.1002/pfi.4140380604

Adebisi, S. A., & Oghojafor, B. E. A. (2012). Evaluating mergers and acquisition as strategic interventions in the Nigerian banking sector: The good, bad, and ugly. *International Business Research, 5*, 147–157. doi:10.5539/ibr.v5n5p147

Adjei-Benin, P., & Sanda, M. (2011). How is the firm dealing with the merger? A study of employee satisfaction with the change process. *Journal of Management and Strategy, 2*(2), 28–37. doi:10.5430/jms.v2n2p28

Agier, I., & Szafarz, A. (2013). Microfinance and gender: Is there a glass ceiling on loan size? *World Development, 42*, 165–181. doi:10.1016/j.worlddev.2012.06.016

Alexandridis, G., Petmezas, D., & Travlos, N. G. (2010). Gains from mergers and acquisitions around the world: New evidence. *Financial Management, 39,* 1671–1695. doi:10.1111/j.1755-053X.2010.01126.x

Al Hawari, M. (2012). A comparative study of trust as a knowledge sharing enabler and its influence on organisational culture. *Journal of Information & Knowledge Management, 11*(2). doi:10.1142/S0219649212500141

Allen, F., & Carletti, E. (2010). An overview of the crisis: Causes, consequences, and solutions. *International Review of Finance, 10,* 1–26. doi:10.1111/j.1468-2443.2009.01103.x

Altinay, L., Riordan, K., & Saunders, M. N. K. (2009). The management of post-merger cultural integration: Implication from the hotel industry. *The Service Industries Journal, 29,* 1359–1375. doi:10.1080/02642060903026213

Amine, L. S., Khan, G. M., Uddin, S. J., & Zaman, M. (2011). The internationalization of an Arab bank: The case of Ahli United Bank of Bahrain. *Thunderbird International Business Review, 53,* 581–600. doi:10.1002/tie.20436

Angwin, D., Gomes, E., Mellahi, K., & Peter, E. (2012). HRM issues and outcomes in African mergers and acquisitions: A study of the Nigerian banking sector. *The International Journal of Human Resource Management, 23,* 2874–2900. doi:10.1080/09 585192.2012.671509

Anifowose, B. D., Atiku, O. S., & Genty, K. I. (2011). The post consolidation of banks: Human resources management challenges and prospects in Nigeria banking sector. *International Journal of Business and Management, 6*(11), 67–75. doi:10.5539/ijbm.v6n11p67

Ashton, J. K. (2012). Do depositors benefit from bank mergers? An examination of the UK deposit market. *International Journal of the Economics of Business*, *19*, 1–23. doi:10.1080/13571516.2 012.642636

Assaf, A. G., Barros, C., & Ibiwoye, A. (2012). Performance assessment of Nigerian banks pre and post consolidation: Evidence from a Bayesian approach. *The Service Industries Journal*, *32*, 215–229. doi:10.1080/02642069.2010.529135

Austin, M. J., & Benton, A. D. (2010). Managing nonprofit mergers: The challenges facing human service organizations. *Administration in Social Work*, *34*, 458–479. doi:10.1080/03643 107.2010.518537

Awasthy, R., Chandrasekaran, V., & Gupta, R. K. (2011). Top-down change in a public sector bank: Lessons from employees' lived-in experiences. *Journal of Indian Business Research*, *3*, 43–62. doi:10.1108/17554191111112460

Azan, W., & Sutter, I. H. (2010). Knowledge transfer in post-merger integration management: Case study of a multinational healthcare company in Greece. *Knowledge Management Research & Practice*, *8*, 307–321. doi:10.1057/kmrp.2010.17

Baker, S. A. (2009). *An examination of bank employees' job satisfaction after a merger and acquisition* (Doctoral dissertation, Northcentral University). Retrieved from http:// gradworks.umi.com/3384714.pdf

Barker, K. J., & Emery, C. R. (2007). Effect of commitment, job involvement and teams on customer satisfaction and profit. *Team Performance Management*, *13*, 90–101. doi:10.1108/13527590710759847

Barth, J., & Jahera, J. (2010). US enacts sweeping financial reform legislation. *Journal of Financial Economic Policy, 2,* 192–195. doi:10.1108/17576381011085412

Bauer, P., & Graf, A. C. (2011). Maximum inflation of the type 1 error rate when sample size and allocation rate are adapted in a pre-planned interim look. *Statistics in Medicine Journal, 30,* 1637–1647. doi:10.1002/sim.4230

Bauer, P., Glimm, E., Graf, A. C., & Koenig, F. (2014). Maximum type 1 error rate inflation in multiarmed clinical trials with adaptive interim sample size modifications. *Biometrical Journal, 56,* 614–630. doi:10.1002/bimj.201300153

Beccalli, E., & Frantz, P. (2009). M&A operations and performance in banking. *Journal of Financial Services Research, 36,* 203–226. doi:10.1007/s10693-008-0051-6

Beccalli, E., & Frantz, P. (2012). The determinants of mergers and acquisitions in banking. *Journal of Financial Services Research, 43,* 265–291. doi:10.1007/s10693-012-0138-y

Beck, T., Levine, R., & Levkov, A. (2010). Big bad banks? The winners and losers from bank deregulation in the United States. *The Journal of Finance, 65,* 1637–1667. doi:10.1111/j.1540-6261.2010.01589.x

Beck, C. T., & Polit, D. F. (2010). Generalization in quantitative and qualitative research: Myths and strategies. *International Journal of Nursing Studies, 47,* 1451–1458. doi:10.1016/j.ijnurstu.2010.06.004

Beebe, A., Blaylock, A., & Sweetser, K. D. (2009). Job satisfaction in public relations internships. *Public Relations Review, 35,* 156–158. doi:10.1016/j.pubrev.2008.09.016

Behr, A., & Heid, F. (2011). The success of bank mergers revisited. An assessment based on a matching strategy. *Journal of Empirical Finance*, *18*, 117–135. doi:10.1016/j.jempfin.2010.08.006

Bellou, V. (2007). Psychological contract assessment after a major organizational change: The case of mergers and acquisitions. *Employee Relations*, *29*, 68–88. doi:10.1108/01425450710714487

Bendeck, Y. M., & Waller, E, R. (2011). Consolidation, concentration, and valuation in the banking industry. *Journal of Business & Economics Research*, *9*(8), 43–50. Retrieved from http://cluteonline.com/journals/index.php/JBER/article/view/5293

Ben Slama, M., Fedhila, H., & Saidane, D. (2012). How to identify targets in the M&A banking operations? Case of cross-border strategies in Europe by line of activity. *Review of Quantitative Finance and Accounting*, *38*, 209–240. doi:10.1007/s11156-010-0224-x

Bernard, C., Fuentelsaz, L., & Gómez, J. (2010). The effect of mergers and acquisitions on productivity: An empirical application to Spanish banking. *Omega*, *38*, 283–293. doi:10.1016/j.omega.2009.07.005

Bernile, G., Lyandres, E., & Zhdanov, A. (2011). A theory of strategic mergers. *Review of Finance*, *16*, 517–575. doi:10.1093/rof/rfr013

Bhal, K. T., Bhaskar, A. U., & Mishra, B. (2012). Strategic HR integration and proactive communication during M&A: A study of Indian bank mergers. *Global Business Review*, *13*, 407–419. doi:10.1177/097215091201300304

Bhaskar, A. U. (2012). HR as business partner during mergers and acquisitions: The key to success is to get involved early. *Human Resource Management International Digest*, *20*(2), 22–23. doi:10.1108/09670731211208157

Bhuyan, R., Ng, S. A.-L., & Vaziri, M. (2010). Do acquisitions create value? Evidence from the US and European bank acquisitions during financial crisis. *Investment Management and Financial Innovations*, *7*(4), 8–25. Retrieved from http://businessperspectives.org/journals_free/imfi/2010/imfi_en_2010_04_Bhuyan.pdf

Bjorkman, I., Sarala, R., Stahl, G. K., & Vaara, E. (2010). The impact of organizational and national cultural differences on social conflict and knowledge transfer in international acquisitions. *Journal of Management Studies*, *49*, 1–27. doi:10.1111/j.1467-6486.2010.00975.x

Boateng, A., & Uddin, M. (2011). Explaining the trends in the UK cross-border mergers and acquisitions: An analysis of macro-economic factors. *International Business Review*, *20*, 547–556. doi:10.1016/j.ibusrev.2010.11.003

Borujeni, H. Z., Chiappa, G. D., Jafari, J., & Khalilzadeh, J. (2013). Methodological approaches to job satisfaction measurement in hospital firms. *International Journal of Contemporary Hospitality Management*, *25*, 865–882. doi:10.1108/IJCHM-05-2012-0067

Brakman, S., Garretsen, H., Marrewijk, C. V., & Witteloostuijn, A. V. (2013). Cross-border merger and acquisition activity and revealed comparative advantage in manufacturing industries. *Journal of Economics & Management Strategy*, *22*, 28–57. Retrieved from http://onlinelibrary.wiley.com/doi/10.1111/jems.12007/abstract

Brewer, E., & Jagtiani, J. (2011). How much did banks pay to become too-big-to-fail and to become systemically important. *Journal of Financial Services Research*, *43*, 1–35. doi:10.1007/s10693-011-0119-6

Brown, K. C., Maples, E. H., Nabirye, R. C., & Pryor, E. R. (2011). Occupational stress, job satisfaction, and job performance among hospital nurses in Kampala, Uganda. *Journal of Nursing Management, 19,* 760–768. doi:10.1111/j.1365-2834.2011.01240.x

Buch, C. M., Koch, C. T., & Koetter, M. (2013). Do banks benefit from internationalization? Revisiting the market power-risk nexus. *Review of Finance, 17,* 1401–1435. doi:10.1093/rof/rfs033

Buchner, A., Erdfelder, E., Faul, F., & Lang, A. (2009). Statistical power analyses using G*Power 3.1: Tests for correlation and regression analyses. *Behavior Research Methods, 41,* 1149–1160. doi:10.3758/BRM.41.4.1149

Calipha, R., Tarba, S., & Brock, D. (2010). Mergers and acquisitions: A review of phases, motives, and success factors. *Advances in Mergers and Acquisitions, 9,* 1–24. doi:10.1108/s1479-361x(2010)0000009004

Carr, C., & Collis, D. (2011, September). Should you have a global strategy? *MIT Sloan Management Review, 53*(1), 21–24. Retrieved from http://sloanreview.mit.edu/the-magazine/2011-fall/53103/

Carr, R. A., Sanders, D. S. A., & Simmons, E. J. V. (2011). Current experience and attitudes to biomedical scientist cut-up: Results of an online survey of UK consultant histopathologists. *Journal of Clinical Pathology, 64,* 363–366. doi:10.1136/jcp.2011.088955

Chaudhary, T., Kaushik, K. P., & Sinha, N. (2010). Measuring post-merger and acquisition performance: An investigation of select financial sector organizations in India. *International Journal of Economics and Finance, 2*(4), 190–200. doi:10.5539/ijef.v2n4p190

Chen, H., Gu, J., Ke, W., Liu, H., & Wei, K. K. (2010). The role of institutional pressures and organizational culture in the firm's intention to adopt internet-enabled supply chain management systems. *Journal of Operations Management, 28,* 372–384. doi:10.1016/j.jom.2009.11.010

Chen, M., Lien, C., & Lin, G. (2011). Modelling job stress as a mediating role in predicting turnover intention. *The Service Industries Journal*, *8*, 1327–1345. doi:10.1080/02642060903437543

Chu, K. H. (2010). Bank mergers, branch networks and economic growth: Theory and evidence from Canada, 1889–1926. *Journal of Macroeconomics*, *32*(1), 265–283. doi:10.1016/j.jmacro.2009.10.006

Cleare, L. (2013). Personality as a predictor of job satisfaction: Study of the relationship between personality and job satisfaction amongst workers in the Bahamas. *Journal of Management Research*, *5*(3), 200–229. doi:10.5296/jmr.v5i3.3936

Colman, H. L., & Lunnan, R. (2010). Organizational identification and serendipitous value creation in post-acquisition integration. *Journal of Management*, *37*, 839–860. doi:10.1177/0149206309354645

Crawford, C. (2011). The repeal of the Glass-Steagal act and the current financial crisis. *Journal of Business & Economics Research*, *9*, 127–133. Retrieved from www.cluteinstitute.com/ojs/index.php/JBER/article/view/949

Crawford, E. R., Lepine, J. A., & Rich, B. L. (2010). Job engagement: Antecedents and effects on job performance. *Academy of Management Journal*, *53*, 617–635. doi:10.5465/AMJ.2010.51468988

Creasy, T., Stull, M., & Peck, S. (2010). Understanding employee-level dynamics within the merger and acquisition process. *Journal of General Management*, *35*(2), 21–42. Retrieved from http://www.researchgate.net/publication/259674443_Understanding_employee-level_dynamics_within_the_merger_and_acquisition_process

Creswell, J. W. (2013). *Research design: Qualitative, quantitative, and mixed methods approaches.* Thousand Oaks, CA: Sage.

Croasdale, K., & Stretcher, R. (2011). Community banks: Surviving unprecedented financial reform. *Academy of Banking Studies Journal, 10*(2), 67–85. Retrieved from http://connection.ebscohost.com/c/articles/64925112/community-banks-surviving-unprecedented-financial-reform

Daly, B. J., Hall, M. A., & Madigan, E. A. (2010). Use of anecdotal notes by clinical nursing faculty: A descriptive study. *Journal of Nursing Education, 49*, 156–159. doi:10.3928/01484834-20090915-03

Dauber, D. (2012). Opposing positions in M&A research: Culture, integration and performance. *Cross Cultural Management: An International Journal, 19*, 375–398. doi:10.1108/13527601211247107

Decock, R., Delobelle, P., Depoorter, A. M., Malatsi, I., Ntuli, S., & Rawlinson, J. L. (2010). Job satisfaction and turnover intent of primary healthcare nurses in rural South Africa: A questionnaire survey. *Journal of Advanced Nursing, 67*, 371–383. doi:10.1111/j.1365-2648.2010.05496.x

De Lange, A. H., Dikkers, J. S. E., Jansen, P. G. W., & Kooij, D. T. A. M. (2010). The influence of age on the associations between HR practices and both affective commitment and job satisfaction: A meta-analysis. *Journal of Organizational Behavior, 31*, 1111–1136. doi:10.1002/job.666

Dollery, B., Villano, R., & Wijeweera, A. (2010). Economic growth and FDI inflows: A stochastic frontier analysis. *The Journal of Developing Areas, 43*(2), 143–158. doi:10.1353/jda.0.0059

do Monte, P. A. (2012). Job dissatisfaction and labour turnover: Evidence from Brazil. *The International Journal of Human*

Resource Management, 23, 1717–1735. doi:10.1080/09585192. 2011.605071

Dylla, J. M., Howard, R., Mickan, S., Sum, J. C., Tilson, J. K., Zibell, M. (2014). Promoting physical therapists' use of research evidence to inform clinical practice: Part 2—A mixed methods evaluation of the PEAK program. *BMC Medical Education, 14*, 126. doi:10.1186/1472-6920-14-126

Ebimobowei, A., & Sophia, J. M. (2011). Mergers and acquisitions in the Nigerian banking industry: An explorative investigation. *The Social Sciences, 6*(3), 213–220. doi:10.3923/sscience.2011.213.220

Erel, I., Liao, R. C., & Weisbach, M. S. (2012). Determinants of cross-border mergers and acquisitions. *The Journal of Finance, 67*, 1045–1082. doi:10.1111/j.1540-6261.2012.01741.x

Evripidou, L. (2012). M&As in the airline industry: Motives and systematic risk. *International Journal of Organizational Analysis, 20*, 435–446. doi:10.1108/19348831211268625

Fassin, Y., & Gosselin, D. (2011). The collapse of a European bank in the financial crisis: An analysis from stakeholder and ethical perspectives. *Journal of Business Ethics, 102*, 169–191. doi:10.1007/s10551-011-0812-2

Fethi, M. D., Kumbhakar, S. C., Lozano-Vivas, A., & Shaban, M. (2011). Consolidation in the European banking industry: How effective is it? *Journal of Productivity Analysis, 36*, 247–261. doi:10.1007/s11123-011-0212-8

Gaganis, C., Pasiouras, F., & Tanna, S., (2011). What drives acquisitions in the EU banking industry? The role of bank regulation and supervision framework, bank specific and market specific factors. *Financial Markets, Institutions, and Instruments, 20*, 29–77. doi:10.1111/j.1468-0416.2011.00165.x

Garbuio, M., Horn, J., & Lovallo, D. (2010). Overcoming biases in M&A: A process perspective. In C. L. Cooper & S. Finkelstein (Eds.), *Advances in Mergers & Acquisitions* (Vol. 9, pp. 83–104). doi:10.1108/s1479-361x(2010)0000009007

García-Suaza, A. F., & Gómez-González, J. E. (2010). The competing risks of acquiring and being acquired: Evidence from Colombia's financial sector. *Economic Systems, 34*, 437–449. doi:10.1016/j.ecosys.2009.11.004

Georgiades, G., & Georgiades, S. (2014). The impact of an acquisition on the employees of the acquired company. *Journal of Business and Economics, 5,* 101-112. Available at http://www.academicstar.us

Ghobadian, A., Hitt, M. A., Kling, G., O'Regan, N., & Weitzel, U. (2014). The effects of cross-border and cross-industry mergers and acquisitions on home-region and global multinational enterprises. *British Journal of Management, 25*, S116–S132. doi:10.1111/1467-8551.12023

Giessner, S. R., Ullrich, J., & van Dick, R. (2011). Social identity and corporate mergers. *Social and Personality Psychology Compass, 5*, 333–345. doi:10.1111/j.1751-9004.2011.00357.x

Goto, N., Nogata, D., & Uchida, K. (2011). Is corporate governance important for regulated firms' shareholders? *Journal of Economics and Business, 63*(1), 46–68. doi:10.1016/j.jeconbus.2010.08.002

Green, S. B., & Salkind, N. J. (2010). *Using SPSS for Windows and Macintosh: Analyzing and understanding data.* Upper Saddle, NJ: Pearson Education.

Ha, J. C., & Ha, R. R. (2011). *Integrative statistics for the social and behavioral sciences.* Seattle, WA: Sage.

Hackbarth, D., & Miao, J. (2012). The dynamics of mergers and acquisitions in oligopolistic industries. *Journal of Economic Dynamics and Control, 36*, 585–609. doi:10.1016/j. jedc.2011.12.001

Hagendorff, J., & Vallascas, F. (2011). The impact of European bank mergers on bidder default risk. *Journal of Banking and Finance, 35*, 902–915. doi:10.1016/j.jbankfin.2010.09.001

Hankir, Y., Rauch, C., & Umber, M. P. (2011). Bank M&A: A market power story? *Journal of Banking & Finance, 35*, 2341–2354. doi:10.1016/j.jbankfin.2011.01.030

Hargie, O., & Tourish, D. (2012). Metaphors of failure and the failures of metaphor: A critical study of root metaphors used by bankers in explaining the banking crisis. *Organization Studies, 33*, 1045–1069. doi:10.1177/0170840612453528

Haslam, S. A., Reynolds, K, J., & Reicher, S. D. (2012). Identity, influence, and change: Rediscovering John Turner's vision for social psychology. *British Journal of Social Psychology, 51*, 201–218. doi:10.1111/j.2044-8309.2011.02091.x

Harada, K., & Ito, T. (2011). Did mergers help Japanese mega-banks avoid failure? Analysis of the distance to default of banks. *Journal of the Japanese and International Economies, 25*(1), 1–22. doi:10.1016/j.jjie.2010.09.001

He, Y., & Zhao, R. (2014). The accounting implication of banking deregulation: An event study of Gramm-Leach-Bliley Act (1999). *Review of Quantitative Finance and Accounting, 42*, 449–468. doi:10.1007/s11156-013-0349-9

Heiney, J. N. (2011). Consolidation in the U.S. banking industry since Riegle-Neal. *Journal of Business & Economics Research, 9*(9), 71–78. Retrieved from http://journals.cluteonline.com/index. php/JBER/article/view/5638

Herrington, R., & Starkweather, J. (2014). *Research and statistical support. University of North Texas computing and information technology center.* Retrieved from www.unt.edu/rss/ Applications.htm

Hoberg, G., & Phillips, G. (2010). Product market synergies and competition in mergers and acquisitions: A text-based analysis. *Review of Financial Studies, 23,* 3773–3811. doi:10.1093/rfs/ hhq053

Holland, W., & Salama, A. (2010). Organisational learning through international M&A integration strategies. *The Learning Organization, 17,* 268–283. doi:10.1108/09696471011034946

Huang, Z., & Marquis, C. (2010). Acquisitions as exaptation: The legacy of founding institutions in the U.S. commercial banking industry. *Academy of Management Journal, 53,* 1441–1473. doi:10.5465/AMJ.2010.57318393

Huyghebaert, N., & Luypaert, M. (2013). Sources of synergy realization in mergers and acquisitions: Empirical evidence from non-serial acquirers in Europe. *International Journal of Financial Research, 4*(2), 49–67. doi:10.5430/ijfr.v4n2p49

Idle, M., & Speculand, B. (2012). When an organisation fails: Lessons from Stafford and beyond. *Faculty Dental Journal, 3,* 134–138. doi:10.1308/204268512x13376834221479

Jharkharia, S. (2012). Supply chain issues in mergers and acquisitions: A case from Indian aviation industry. *International Journal of Aviation Management, 1*(4), 293–303. doi:10.1504/ IJAM.2012.050476

Jog, V., & Zhu, P. (2012). Impact on target firm risk-return characteristics of domestic and cross-border mergers and acquisitions in emerging markets. *Emerging Markets Finance and Trade, 48*(4), 79–101. doi:10.2753/REE1540-496x480405

Kalpic, B. (2008). Why bigger is not always better: The strategic logic of value creation through M&As. *Journal of Business Strategy, 29*(6), 4–13. doi:10.1108/02756660810917183

Karunaratne, C., & Wickramasinghe, V. (2009). People management in mergers and acquisitions in Sri Lanka: Employee perceptions. *The International Journal of Human Resource Management, 20*, 694–715. doi:10.1080/09585190802707508

Kaur, G., & Singh, J. (2011). Customer satisfaction and universal banks: An empirical study. *International Journal of Commerce and Management, 21*, 327–348. doi:10.1108/10569211111189356

Kim, Y. (2011). Confucianism-based organization value & post-merger syndrome in cross-border M&A: How family-system principle hinders communication in cross-border M&A. *International Journal of Business and Management, 6*(4), 49–63. doi:10.5539/ijbm.v6n4p49

Kitamura, T., Sakata, M., & Takagishi, Y. (2012). Influence of the municipal merger on local government employees' stress response in Japan. *Industrial Health, 50*, 132–141. doi:10.2486/indhealth.MS1290

Konstantopoulos, N., Sakas, D., & Triantafyllopoulos, Y. (2009). Lessons from a case study for Greek banking M&A negotiations. *Management Decisions, 47*, 1300–1312. doi:10.1108/00251740910984550

Krishnaswamy, O. R., & Satyaprasad, B. G. (2010). *Business research methods*. Mumbai, India: Himalaya Publishing House.

Krochalk, P. C., & Snarr, C. E. (1996). Job satisfaction and organizational characteristics: Results of a nationwide survey of baccalaureate nursing faculty in the United States. *Journal of Advanced Nursing, 24*, 405–412. doi:10.1046/j.1365-2648.1996.19725.x

Krug, J. A. (2009). Brain drain: Why top management bolts after M&As. *Journal of Business Strategy, 30*(6), 4–14. doi:10.1108/02756660911003077

Kumar, N., Pak, O. G., & Rose, R. C. (2009). The effect of organizational learning on organizational commitment, job satisfaction and work performance. *Journal of Applied Business Research, 25*(6), 55–66. Retrieved from http://connection. ebscohost.com/c/articles/45585971/effect-organizational-learning-organizational-commitment-job-satisfaction-work-performance

Kusstatscher, V., Sinkovics, R. R., & Zagelmeyer, S. (2011). Between merger and syndrome: The intermediary role of emotions in four cross-border M&As. *International Business Review, 20*, 27–47. doi:10.1016/j.ibusrev.2010.05.002

Lahovnik, M. (2011). Strategic fit between business strategies in the post-acquisition period and acquisition performance. *Journal for East European Management Studies, 16*, 358–370. Retrieved from http://EconPapers.repec.org/ R e P E c : r a i : j o e e m s : d o i _ 1 0 . 1 6 8 8 / 1 8 6 2 - 0 0 1 9 _ jeems_2011_04_lahovnik

Lambkin, M. C., & Muzellec, L. (2010). Leveraging brand equity in business-to-business mergers and acquisitions. *Industrial Marketing Management, 39*, 1234–1239. doi:10.1016/j. indmarman.2010.02.020

Lee, C., Lee, H., & Wu, C. (2009). Factors that influence employees' organizational identity after M&A: The acquirer and acquired perspective. *African Journal of Business Management, 3*, 695–704. Retrieved from http://www.academicjournals.org/article/ article1380560409_Lee%20et%20al..pdf

Li, S., Qiu, J., & Wan, C. (2011). Corporate globalization and bank lending. *Journal of International Business Studies, 42*, 1016–1042. doi:10.1057/jibs.2011.29

Liargovas, P., & Repousis, S. (2011). The impact of mergers and acquisitions on the performance of the Greek banking sector: An event study approach. *International Journal of Economics and Finance, 3*(2), 89–100. doi:10.5539/ijef.v3n2p89

Malul, M., Meydani, A., & Shoham, A. (2012). Acquisitions, market share, and interest\groups. *European Journal of International Management, 6*(4), 442–457. doi:10.1504/EJIM.2012.048157

Markham, J. W. (2010). Lessons for competition law from the economic crisis: The prospect for antitrust responses to the "too-big-to-fail" phenomenon. University of San Francisco Law (Research Paper No. 2011-15). Retrieved from http://papers.ssrn.com/sol3/papers.cfm?abstract_id=1634839

Marks, M. L., & Mirvis, P. H. (2011). Merge ahead: A research agenda to increase merger and acquisition success. *Journal of Business and Psychology, 26*, 161–168. doi:10.1007/s10869-011-9219-4

Mehrotra, V., Spronk, J., Steenbeek, O., & van Schaik, D. (2011). Creditor-focused corporate governance: Evidence from mergers and acquisitions in Japan. *Journal of Financial and Quantitative Analysis, 46*, 1051–1088. doi:10.1017/s002210901100024x

Mili, M., & Sahut, J. (2011). Banking distress in MENA countries and the role of mergers as a strategic policy to resolve distress. *Economic Modelling, 28*, 138–146. doi:10.1016/j.econmod.2010.09.017

Muhammad, U. K. (2011). Post-merger profitability: A case of Royal Bank of Scotland (RBS). *International Journal of Business and Social Science, 2*, 2011. Retrieved from http://www.ijbssnet.com/journals/Vol._2_No._5_[Special_Issue_-_March_2011]/20.pdf

Muijs, D. (2004). *Doing quantitative research in education with SPSS*. London, England: Sage Publications Inc.

Mylonakis, J. (2006). The perception of banks' mergers and acquisitions by bank employees. *Financial Services Management*, *1*, 205–214. Retrieved from http://www.inderscience.com/info/inarticle.php?artid=9626

Nadiri, H., & Tanova, C. (2010). An investigation of the role of justice in turnover intentions, job satisfaction, and organizational citizenship behavior in hospitality industry. *International Journal of Hospitality Management*, *29*, 33–41. doi:10.1016/j.ijhm.2009.05.001

Okoro, H. M. (2010). *The relationship between organizational culture and performance: merger in the Nigerian banking industry* (Doctoral dissertation). Available from ProQuest Dissertations and Theses database. (UMI No. 3424825)

Olowe, R. (2011). The impact of the 2004 bank capital announcement on the Nigerian stock market. *African Journal of Economic and Management Studies*, *2*, 180–201. doi:10.1108/20400701111176694

Papaioannou, G. (2011). Competing for underwriting market share: The case of commercial banks and securities firms. *Journal of Financial Services Marketing*, *16*, 153–169. doi:10.1057/fsm.2011.12

Peloquin, J. (2011). *An investigative case study of human capital in mergers and acquisitions* (Doctoral dissertation). Available from ProQuest Dissertations and Theses database. (UMI No. 3443646)

Phillips, G. M., & Zhdanov, A. (2013). R&D and the incentives from merger and acquisition activity. *Review of Financial Studies Journal*, *26*, 34–78. doi:10.1093/rfs/hhs109

Piskula, T. J. (2011). Governance and merger activity in banking. *The Journal of Business and Economic Studies*, *17*(1), 1–15. Retrieved from http://ssrn.com/abstract=1909271

Prasch, R. E. (2012). The Dodd-Frank Act: Financial reform or business as usual? *Journal of Economic Issues*, *46*, 549–556. (Accession No. 76169473)

Roth, G., & Shook, K. L. (2011). Downsizings, mergers, and acquisitions: Perspectives of human resource development practitioners. *Journal of European Industrial Training*, *35*, 135–153. doi:10.1108/03090591111109343

Sagner, J. S. (2012). M&A failures: Receivables and inventory may be keys. *Journal of Corporate Accounting and Finance*, *23*(2), 21–25. doi:10.1002/jcaf.21733

Samet, K. (2010). Banking and value creation in emerging market. *International Journal of Economics and Finance*, *2*(5), 66–78. doi:10.5539/ijef.v2n5p66

Sarala, R, M., & Vaara, E. (2010). Cultural differences, convergence, and crossvergence as explanations of knowledge transfer in international acquisitions. *Journal of International Business Studies*, *41*, 1365–1390. doi:10.1057/jibs.2009.89

Schmidt, I. (2011). [Review of the book *The ABCs of economic crisis: What working people need to know*, by F. Magdoff & M. D. Yates]. *Labour/Le Travail*, *68*, 238–240. Retrieved from http://muse.jhu.edu/journals/labour_le_travail/summary/v068/68.schmidt.html

Schmidts, T., & Shepherd, D. (2013). Social identity theory and the family business: A contribution to understanding family business dynamics. *Small Enterprise Research*, *20*, 76–86. doi:10.5172/ser.2013.20.2.76

116

Schroeder, H. (2012). Post-merger integration the art and science way. *Strategic HR Review, 11,* 272–277. doi:10.1108/14754391211248684

Shull, B. (2010). *Too big to fail in financial crises: Motives, countermeasures, and prospects* (Levy Economics Institute Working Paper No. 601). doi:10.2139/ssm.1621909

Sperduto, V. (2007). *The impact of the appreciative inquiry summit process on employee engagement and organizational culture in a merger and acquisition* (Doctoral dissertation). Available from ProQuest Dissertations and Theses database. (UMI No. 3258978)

Springer, G. J. (2010). *Job motivation, satisfaction, and performance among bank employees: A correlational study* (Doctoral dissertation). Available from ProQuest Dissertations and Theses database. (UMI No. 3429116)

Stacy, M. (2010). The wearing-off phenomenon and the use of questionnaires to facilitate its recognition in Parkinson's disease. *Journal of Neural Transmission, 117,* 837–846. doi:10.1007/s00702-010-0424-5

Steigner, T., & Sutton, N. K. (2011). How does national culture impact internationalization benefits in cross-border mergers and acquisitions? *The Financial Review, 46,* 103–125. doi:10.1111/j.1540-6288.2010.00292.x

Tarba, S., & Weber, Y. (2011). Exploring integration approach in related mergers: Post-merger integration in the high-tech industry. *International Journal of Organizational Analysis, 19,* 202–221. doi:10.1108/19348831111149178

Teerikangas, S. (2010). Dynamics of acquired firm pre-acquisition employee reactions. *Journal of Management, 38,* 599–639. doi:10.1177/0149206310383908

Tudor, T. R. (2011). Motivating employees with limited pay incentives using equity theory and the fast-food industry as a model. *International Journal of Business and Social Science*, *2*(23), 95–101. Retrieved from http://ijbssnet.com/journals/ Vol_2_No_23_Special_Issue_December_2011/11.pdf

Vives, X. (2011). Competition policy in banking. *Oxford Review of Economic Policy, 27*, 479–497. doi:10.1093/oxrep/grr021

Wheelock, D. C., & Wilson, P. W. (2012). Do large banks have lower costs? New estimates of return to scale for U.S. banks. *Journal of Money, Credit, and Banking, 44*, 171–199. doi:10.1111/j.1538-4616.2011.00472.x

Whitaker, M. K. (2011). *Dimensions of organizational culture during a merger: quantitative perspective from non-managerial employees* (Doctoral dissertation). Available from ProQuest Dissertations and Theses database. (UMI No. 3439660)

Willig, C. (2013). *Introducing qualitative research in psychology.* Berkshire, England: McGraw-Hill Education.

Appendix A: Questionnaire

PLEASE PROVIDE THE FOLLOWING IDENTIFICATION INFORMATION

1. How long have you worked for this organization?

    (a) less than 2 years (b) 2 to less than 4 years

    (c) 4 to less than 6 years

    (d) 6 to less than 10 years (e) 10 years or more

2. What is your age?

    (a) under 25 years (b) 25 to 35 years (c) 36 to 45 years

    (d) 46 to 55 Years (e) 56 to 65 years (f) Over 65 years

3. What is your job level?

    (a) Professional Teller/Semi-skilled

    (b) Personal Banker, Small Business Specialist, Sales & Service Specialist

    (c) Teller Operations Specialist, Assistant Manager, Office Manager, Administrative Assistant, Banking Center Manager

    (d) Consumer Market Manager, Regional Manager, Area Executive

    (e) CEO, President, Executive Vice President (f) Others

4. What is your gender?

   (a) Male (b) Female

5. What is your race?

   (a) White (b) African American/Black (c) Hispanic

   (d) Non-Hispanic or white

   (e) Others

6. What is the level of education you have completed?

   (a) High School/GED (b) Associate Degree

   (d) Bachelor's Degree (e) Master's Degree or Higher

If you were an employee of the bank during and after any of the bank's mergers and acquisitions (M&A), respond to the following questions, based on how each demographic factor affected your job satisfaction or job security, if any.

On a scale of 1 – 10, with 1 as the lowest & 10 as the highest score:

7. How did your job tenure affect your job satisfaction after the M&A?

   1 2 3 4 5 6 7 8 9 10

8. How did your race affect your job satisfaction after the M&A?

   1 2 3 4 5 6 7 8 9 10

9. How did your age affect your job satisfaction after the M&A?

   1 2 3 4 5 6 7 8 9 10

10. How did your gender affect your job satisfaction after the M&A?

    1 2 3 4 5 6 7 8 9 10

11. How did your level of education affect your job satisfaction after the M&A?

    1 2 3 4 5 6 7 8 9 10

12. How did your job level (position or title) affect your job satisfaction after the M&A?

    1 2 3 4 5 6 7 8 9 10

Abridged Job Descriptive Index

Work on Present Job

13. Think of the work you do at present. How well does each of the following words or phrases describe your work? On the blank beside each word or phrase below, write:

    Y for "Yes" if it describes your work

    N for "No" if it does not describe it

    Question mark (?) for if you cannot decide

    __ Fascinating
    __ Routine
    __ Satisfying
    __ Boring
    __ Good
    __ Gives sense of accomplishment
    __ Respected
    __ Exciting
    __ Rewarding
    __ Useful

___ Challenging
___ Simple
___ Repetitive
___ Creative
___ Dull
___ Uninteresting
___ Can see results
___ Uses my abilities

Pay

14. Think of the pay you get now. How well does each of the following words or phrases describe your present pay? On the blank beside each word or phrase below, write:

Y for "Yes" if it describes your pay

N for "No" if it does not describe it

Question mark (?) for if you cannot decide

___ Income adequate for normal expenses
___ Fair
___ Barely live on income
___ Bad
___ Comfortable
___ Less than I deserve
___ Well paid
___ Enough to live on
___ Underpaid

Opportunities for Promotion

15. Think of the opportunities for promotion that you have now. How well does each of the following words or phrases describe these? On the blank beside each word or phrase below, write:

Y for "Yes" if it describes your opportunities for promotion

N for "No" if it does not describe them

Question mark (?) for if you cannot decide

__ Good opportunities for promotion
__ Opportunities somewhat limited
__ Promotion on ability
__ Regular promotions
__ Good chance for promotion
__ Fairly good chance for promotion
__ Infrequent promotions
__ Very limited
__ Dead-end job

Supervision

16. Think of the kind of supervision that you get on your job. How well does each of the following words or phrases describe this? On the blank beside each word or phrase below, write:

Y for "Yes" if it describes the supervision you get on the job

N for "No" if it does not describe it

Question mark (?) for if you cannot decide

__ Supportive
__ Hard to please
__ Impolite
__ Praises good work
__ Tactful
__ Influential
__ Up-to-date
__ Unkind
__ Has favorites

___ Tells me where I stand
___ Annoying
___ Stubborn
___ Knows job well
___ Bad
___ Intelligent
___ Poor planner
___ Around when needed
___ Lazy

People on Your Present Job

17. Think of the majority of people with whom you work or meet in connection with your work. How well does each of the following words or phrases describe these people? On the blank beside each word or phrase below, write:

Y for "Yes" if it describes the people with whom you work

N for "No" if it does not describe them

Question mark (?) for if you cannot decide

___ Stimulating
___ Boring
___ Slow
___ Helpful
___ Stupid
___ Responsible
___ Likeable
___ Intelligent
___ Easy to make enemies
___ Rude
___ Smart
___ Lazy
___ Unpleasant
___ Supportive

___ Active
___ Narrow interests
___ Frustrating
___ Stubborn

Job in General (JIG)

18. Think of your job in general. All in all, what is it like most of the time? On the blank beside each word or phrase below, write:

    Y for "Yes" if it describes your job

    N for "No" if it does not describe it

    Question mark (?) for if you cannot decide

    ___ Pleasant
    ___ Bad
    ___ Waste of time
    ___ Good
    ___ Undesirable
    ___ Worthwhile
    ___ Worse than most
    ___ Acceptable
    ___ Superior
    ___ Better than most
    ___ Disagreeable
    ___ Makes me content
    ___ Inadequate
    ___ Excellent
    ___ Rotten
    ___ Enjoyable
    ___ Poor

Appendix B:
Email Invitation to Participants

Dear _____,

My name is Michael Madu. I am currently a Doctor of Business Administration (DBA) student at Walden University.

My research study focuses on examining why top talents, including leaders leave the bank after a merger and acquisition. I will examine this problem from the perspectives of job tenure, race, gender, age, education, and job level or position. I will be looking to see if any of these elements has any bearing to your job satisfaction and your decision to stay or leave the bank after the merger and acquisition.

To help me complete this project, I am requesting for you to access and complete the survey I have posted on surveymonkey.com by clicking on the link https://www.research.net/s/MaduWaldenUniversity.

Participation is optional and your identity and that of the bank will be completely anonymous. Your contribution could help to improve associate satisfaction and retention after a merger and acquisition.

The survey takes about ten minutes to complete. I will send follow-up e-mail within one week as a reminder that you have seven more days to complete the survey.

If you have any question, please feel free to reach me at 215-531-4178 (Phone) or e-mail me at madumc2012@yahoo.com

Thank you.

Michael C. Madu
Doctor of Business Administration Student
Walden University

Appendix C:
The Follow-up Invitation E-mail

I sent an e-mail to you about a week ago, requesting you to complete a survey I posted on SurveyMonkey®. I wish to thank those of you that already participated.

This is a reminder that you still have seven days left to participate, if you wish. To help me complete this project, I am requesting for you to access and complete the survey I have posted on surveymonkey.com by clicking on the link https://www.research. net/s/MaduWaldenUniversity

As a bank employee, this research has the potential to benefit you. The research focuses on examining the factors that affect the job satisfaction of bank employees after a merger and acquisition.

Thank you.

Michael C. Madu
Doctor of Business Administration Student
Walden University

Appendix D:
Permission to use the JDI and AJIG Scales

Bowling Green State University

Job Descriptive Index
(JDI) Office
214 Psychology Building
Department of Psychology
Bowling Green State University
Bowling Green, OH 43403

January 19, 2012

The Job Descriptive Index (JDI) and family of measures – including the Job In General scale (JiG), abridged Job Descriptive Index (aJDI), abridged Job In General scale (aJiG), Trust in Management scale (TiM), Intent to Quit (ITQ), Stress in General (SiG) scale, Scale of Life Satisfaction (SOLS), and Survey of Work Values, Revised, Form U. (SWV) are owned by Bowling Green State University, copyright 1975-2010.

Permission is hereby granted to **Mike Madu** to use these measures in his or her research.

The aforementioned scales may be administered as many times as needed in this course of this research.

Chris Chang
Chris Chang
JDI Research Assistant
Tel: 419.372.8247
Fax: 419.372.6013
jdi_ra@bgsu.edu

Appendix E: Letter to the Bank

The Chief Executive Officer

_____ Bank

My name is Michael Madu. I am currently a Doctor of Business Administration (DBA) student at Walden University.

I am conducting a research on the Job Satisfaction of Bank Employees after a merger and acquisition, from the perspectives of job tenure, job level or title, level of education, race, age, or gender.

I selected your bank because you went through several mergers in the last ten years and is the most appropriate candidate for this research. In conducting this research, I will send letters of invitation (copy attached) to your managers in all locations in Bucks, Delaware, Montgomery, and Philadelphia counties of Pennsylvania. I will request the managers to forward my letters of invitation to other employees. I intend to collect this data within 14 days. If sufficient sample size is not obtained in the first week, I will be asking the managers to forward reminder notifications to the employees on my behalf. Upon request, a copy of the research results will be provided to you.

The employee can access this survey from his or her home computer. The survey takes about 10 minutes to complete. The name of the bank and identities of the participants will not be disclosed.

In this research, I will examine if the demographic factors mentioned above have any bearing on the job satisfaction of current bank employees and their decisions to stay or leave the bank after the merger and acquisition. The research has the potential to shade light on certain factors that influence the job satisfaction of bank employees after a merger and acquisition. Perhaps, the findings can help bank leaders in managing and executing future mergers in a manner that will be sensitive to the identified factors, and potentially help to maximize the satisfaction and retention of employees, especially the top talents.

Thank you for your support.

Mike Madu
Doctor of Business Administration (DBA) Student
Walden University

Appendix F:
SurveyMonkey® Confidentiality and Security Policy

How do you keep our data secure?

As stated in our privacy policy, we will not use your data for our own purposes.

The data you collect is kept private and confidential. You are the owner of all data collected or uploaded into the survey.

In regards to the security of our infrastructure, here is an overview of our setup.

We do offer SSL encryption for the survey link and survey pages during transmission. The cost is an additional $9.95 per month.

The servers are kept at Inflow - www.inflow.com.

Physical

- Servers kept in locked cage
- Entry requires a pass card and biometric recognition
- Digital surveillance equipment
- Controls for temperature, humidity and smoke/fire detection
- Staffed 24/7

Network

- Multiple independent connections to Tier 1 Internet access providers
- Fully redundant OC-48 SONET Rings
- Uptime monitored every 5 minutes, with escalation to SurveyMonkey® staff
- Firewall restricts access to all ports except 80 (http) and 443 (https)\
- QualysGuard network security audits performed quarterly

Hardware

- Servers have redundant internal power supplies
- Data is on RAID 10, operating system on RAID 1
- Servers are mirrored and can failover in less than one hour

Software

- Code in ASP, running on SQL Server 2000 and Windows 2000 Server
- Latest patches applied to all operating system and application files
- SSL encryption of all billing data
- Data backed up every hour internally
- Data backed up every night to centralized backup system, with offsite backups in event of catastrophe

Source:

Baker, S. A. (2009). *An examination of bank employees' job satisfaction after a merger and acquisition* (Doctoral dissertation). Available from ProQuest Dissertations and Theses database. (UMI No. 3384714)

Appendix G:
Informed Consent Form

You are invited to take part in a research study examining the job satisfaction levels of bank employees after a merger and acquisition. You are invited to participate because you experienced mergers and acquisitions in the past and are in a good position to give honest feedback on how mergers and acquisitions affected you from the perspectives of your job tenure, job position or title, age, race, gender, or level of education.

This research is being conducted by Michael C. Madu, who is a doctoral student at Walden University. Research gathered in this study will be used to explore whether any of the stated demographic factors has any bearing on your job satisfaction and your decision to stay or leave the bank after the merger and acquisition. The findings of the research could contribute to future retention efforts and job satisfaction of bank employees as banks undergo mergers and acquisitions.

Procedures

If you agree to participate in this study, you will be asked to:

- Respond to 18 questions regarding your satisfaction levels on your job after you experienced a merger and acquisition based on your job tenure, job position or title, age, race, gender, or level of education.

- Keep/print a copy of the consent form.

Voluntary Nature of the Study

Your participation in this study is voluntary. Your decision to participate or not participate will be respected. Given that the data collection process is anonymous, once you submit a survey, it will not be possible to isolate and remove your data if you change your mind afterwards. If you feel any question is too personal, you may skip it.

Risks and Benefits of Being in the Study

There are minimal risks in being in the study. This study could contribute to improved retention efforts and job satisfaction of bank employees after a merger and acquisition.

Compensation

Your participation in this study will be highly appreciated by the researcher. No compensation will be given to any participant.

Confidentiality

Any information you provide will be kept confidential. The researcher will not include your name or anything that may disclose your identity in any part of the reports of the study.

Contacts and Questions

If you have any general question at any time, you may contact: Walden University. **Statement of Consent**

To protect your privacy, signatures are not being collected and completion of the survey would indicate your consent, if you choose to participate.

Appendix H:
AJDI/AJIG Scoring Model

AJDI/AJIG Scoring Model

Scale	Abbreviated Score		Multiply		Divide
Pay	Total	x	9	/	5
Promotion	Total	x	9	/	5
Work	Total	x	18	/	5
Supervisor	Total	x	18	/	5
*Co-Worker	Total	x	18	/	5
JIG	Total	x	18	/	8

*Co-Worker = People on Your Present Job
Yes = 1
No = 2
? = 3

Source:

Baker, S. A. (2009). *An examination of bank employees' job satisfaction after a merger and acquisition* (Doctoral dissertation). Available from ProQuest Dissertations and Theses database. (UMI No. 3384714)

Appendix I:
JDI Office – Terms of Use

A. Consent to use of an electronic signature for accepting the terms of use for JDI-related scales.

The "Electronic Signatures in Global and National Commerce Act" requires that individuals provide consent to sign electronic records that would otherwise be legally effective only if provided to you as a printed or written paper record. As a result, in order to accept the terms of use for JDI-related scales electronically, you must provide your consent that you have the capability to receive such disclosures and are fully aware of the consequences of agreeing to sign records electronically.

Definitions:

Record - The term "record" means information that is inscribed on a tangible medium or that is stored in an electronic or other medium and is retrievable in perceivable form.

Electronic Record - The term "electronic record" means a contract or other record created, generated, sent, communicated, received, or stored by electronic means.

Electronic Signature - The term "electronic signature" means an electronic sound, symbol, or process, attached to or logically associated with a contract or other record and executed or adopted by a person with the intent to sign the record.

1. Electronic Signatures and Records. Upon accepting the terms below, you are providing your electronic consent to the use of an electronic signature for these terms. In particular, you acknowledge receipt of this notice and consent to the use of an electronic signature for accepting the terms of use for JDI-related scales.

2. Minimum Hardware and Software Requirements. The following are the software requirements to accept the terms of use for JDI-related scales:

    Operating Systems: Windows 98, Windows 2000, Windows XP or Windows Vista; or Macintosh OS 8.1 or higher.

    Browsers: Internet Explorer 5.01 or above or equivalent

    Other Applications: Adobe Acrobat Reader or equivalent for PDF files.

3. Capability to Receive Such Disclosures. Upon accepting the terms below, you will receive a copy of the terms via e-mail in PDF format.

4. 4. Right to NOT USE electronic signatures. Each individual has the right to agree to these terms in paper form. If you choose to sign a paper copy of the terms of use for JDI-related scales, contact the JDI office by phone at (419) 372-8247 or by e-mail at jdi_ra@bgsu.edu.

B. Terms of Use for JDI-related scales (i.e., JDI/JIG, aJDI/aJIG, SIG, and TIM)

1. I understand that the JDI scales provided on this website are owned by BGSU, are proprietary to BGSU and BGSU owns the copyright to these JDI scales.

2. I understand that the JDI scales provided on this website are provided free of charge, but that a valid e-mail address is required for access to and use of the JDI scales. (Note: We respect your privacy and will never distribute or sell your information to any third party.)

3. I understand that the JDI Office may occasionally contact me via e-mail about its products and services.

4. I understand the scales are for my sole use only and will not distribute them to any third party.

5. I understand the scales may not be reprinted or otherwise published in their full form, and I will contact the JDI Office to obtain specific sample items that may be published should the need arise.

6. I understand the scales were developed by researchers at Bowling Green State University and any publication/ presentation involving the scales must include proper and scholarly citation.

7. I understand the scales are intended to be used "as is" without any modifications to the items and/or the scoring procedure.

Appendix J:
SurveyMonkey® Terms of Use

Thanks for using SurveyMonkey's products and services ("**Services**").

These Terms of Use ("**TOU**") contain the terms under which SurveyMonkey and its affiliates provide their Services to you and describe how the Services may be accessed and used.

Depending on which Services you use, additional terms and policies (including rules, guidelines and other similarly named documents) presented with those Services may apply ("**Additional Terms**"). Those Additional Terms become a part of your agreement with us if you use those Services. For example, if you use our survey services, the Survey Terms of Service apply. We refer to the combination of this TOU and any applicable Additional Terms collectively as these "**Terms**".

You indicate your agreement to these Terms by clicking or tapping on a button indicating your acceptance of these Terms, by executing a document that references them, or by using the Services.

If you will be using the Services on behalf of an organization, you agree to these Terms on behalf of that organization and you represent that you have the authority to do so. In such case, "you" and "your" will refer to that organization.

Certain country-specific terms in Section 14.3 may apply to you if you are located outside the United States.

1.1. Fees for Services. You agree to pay to SurveyMonkey any fees for each Service you purchase or use (including any overage fees), in accordance with the pricing and payment terms presented to you for that Service. Where applicable, you will be billed using the billing method you select through your account management page. Fees paid by you are non-refundable, except as provided in these Terms or when required by law.

1.2. Subscriptions. Some of our Services are billed on a subscription basis (we call these "**Subscriptions**"). This means that you will be billed in advance on a recurring, periodic basis (each period is called a "**billing cycle**"). Billing cycles are typically monthly or annual, depending on what subscription plan you select when purchasing a Subscription. **Your Subscription will automatically renew at the end of each billing cycle unless you cancel auto-renewal through your online account management page, or by contacting our customer support team.** While we will be sad to see you go, you may cancel auto-renewal on your Subscription at any time, in which case your Subscription will continue until the end of that billing cycle before terminating. You may cancel auto-renewal on your Subscription immediately after the Subscription starts if you do not want it to renew.

1.3. Taxes. Unless otherwise stated, you are responsible for any taxes (other than SurveyMonkey's income tax) or duties associated with the sale of the Services, including any related penalties or interest (collectively, "**Taxes**"). You will pay SurveyMonkey for the Services without any reduction for Taxes. If SurveyMonkey is obliged to collect or pay Taxes, the Taxes will be invoiced to you, unless you provide SurveyMonkey with a valid tax exemption certificate authorized by the appropriate taxing authority or other documentation providing evidence that no tax should be charged. SurveyMonkey will not charge you VAT if you provide us with a VAT number issued by a taxing authority in the European Union, are purchasing the Services from SurveyMonkey Europe Sarl for business reasons, and are located in a different European Union member state from SurveyMonkey Europe Sarl. If you are required by law to withhold any Taxes from your payments to SurveyMonkey, you must provide SurveyMonkey with an official tax receipt or other appropriate documentation to support such payments.

1.4. Price Changes. SurveyMonkey may change the fees charged for the Services at any time, provided that, for Services billed on a subscription basis, the change will become effective only at the end of the then-current billing cycle of your Subscription. SurveyMonkey will provide you with reasonable prior written notice of any change in fees to give you an opportunity to cancel your Subscription before the change becomes effective.

1.5. Overage Fees. Unless otherwise stated, any overage fees incurred by you will be billed in arrears on a monthly basis. Overage fees which remain unpaid for 30 days after being billed are considered overdue. Failure to pay overage fees when due may result in the applicable Service being limited, suspended, or terminated (subject to applicable legal requirements), which may result in a loss of your data associated with that Service.

2.1. Privacy. In the course of using the Services, you may submit content to SurveyMonkey (including your personal data and the personal data of others) or third parties may submit content to you through the Services (your "**Content**"). We know that by giving us your Content, you are trusting us to treat it appropriately. SurveyMonkey's Privacy Policy, together with any Service-specific data use policies, privacy statements and privacy notices (collectively, "**privacy policies**"), detail how we treat your Content and personal data and we agree to adhere to those privacy policies. You in turn agree that SurveyMonkey may use and share your Content in accordance with our privacy policies.

2.2. Confidentiality. SurveyMonkey will treat your Content as confidential information and only use and disclose it in accordance with these Terms (including our privacy policies). However, your Content is not regarded as confidential information if such Content: (a) is or becomes public (other than through breach of these Terms by SurveyMonkey); (b) was lawfully known to SurveyMonkey before receiving it from you; (c) is received by SurveyMonkey from a third party without knowledge of breach of any obligation owed to you; or (d) was independently developed by SurveyMonkey without reference to your Content.

3.1. You Retain Ownership of Your Content. You retain ownership of all of your intellectual property rights in your Content. SurveyMonkey does not claim ownership over any of your Content. These Terms do not grant us any licenses or rights to your Content except for the limited rights needed for us to provide the Services, and as otherwise described in these Terms.

3.2. Limited License to Your Content. You grant SurveyMonkey a worldwide, royalty free license to use, reproduce, distribute, modify, adapt, create derivative works, make publicly available, and otherwise exploit your Content, but only for the limited purposes of providing the Services to you and as otherwise permitted by SurveyMonkey's privacy policies. This license for such limited purposes continues even after you stop using our Services, though you may have the ability to delete your Content in relation to certain Services such that SurveyMonkey no longer has access to it. This license also extends to any trusted third parties we work with to the extent necessary to provide the Services to you. If you provide SurveyMonkey with feedback about the Services, we may use your feedback without any obligation to you.

3.3. Copyright Claims (DMCA Notices). SurveyMonkey Inc. responds to notices of alleged copyright infringement in accordance with the U.S. Digital Millennium Copyright Act (DMCA). If you believe that your work has been exploited in a way that constitutes copyright infringement, you may notify SurveyMonkey's agent for claims of copyright infringement.

3.4. Other IP Claims. SurveyMonkey respects the intellectual property rights of others, and we expect our users to do the same. If you believe a SurveyMonkey user is infringing upon your intellectual property rights, you may report it through our online form. Claims of copyright infringement should follow the DMCA process outlined in these Terms, or any equivalent process available under local law.

4.1. SurveyMonkey IP. Neither these Terms nor your use of the Services grants you ownership in the Services or the content you access through the Services (other than your Content). Except as permitted by SurveyMonkey's Brand and Trademark Use Policy, these Terms do not grant you any right to use SurveyMonkey's trademarks or other brand elements.

5.1. User Content. The Services display content provided by others that is not owned by SurveyMonkey. Such content is the sole responsibility of the entity that makes it available. Correspondingly, you are responsible for your own Content and you must ensure that you have all the rights and permissions needed to use that Content in connection with the Services. SurveyMonkey is not responsible for any actions you take with respect to your Content, including sharing it publicly. Please do not use content from the Services unless you have first obtained the permission of its owner, or are otherwise authorized by law to do so.

5.2. Content Review. You acknowledge that, in order to ensure compliance with legal obligations, SurveyMonkey may be required to review certain content submitted to the Services to determine whether it is illegal or whether it violates these Terms (such as when unlawful content is reported to us). We may also modify, prevent access to, delete, or refuse to display content that we believe violates the law or these Terms. However, SurveyMonkey otherwise has no obligation to monitor or review any content submitted to the Services.

5.3. Third Party Resources. SurveyMonkey may publish links in its Services to internet websites maintained by third parties. SurveyMonkey does not represent that it has reviewed such third-party websites and is not responsible for them or any content appearing on them. Trademarks displayed in conjunction with the Services are the property of their respective owners.

6.1. Keep Your Password Secure. If you have been issued an account by SurveyMonkey in connection with your use of the Services, you are responsible for safeguarding your password and any other credentials used to access that account. You, and not SurveyMonkey, are responsible for any activity occurring in your account (other than activity that SurveyMonkey is directly responsible for which is not performed in accordance with the Customer's instructions), whether or not you authorized that activity. If you become aware of any unauthorized access to your account, you should notify SurveyMonkey immediately. Accounts may not be shared and may only be used by one individual per account.

6.2. Keep Your Details Accurate. SurveyMonkey occasionally sends notices to the email address registered with your account. You must keep your email address and, where applicable, your contact details and payment details associated with your account current and accurate. Accounts are controlled by the entity whose email address is registered with the account.

6.3. Remember to Backup. You are responsible for maintaining, protecting, and making backups of your Content. To the extent permitted by applicable law, SurveyMonkey will not be liable for any failure to store, or for loss or corruption of, your Content.

6.4. Account Inactivity. SurveyMonkey may terminate your account and delete any content contained in it if there is no account activity (such as a log in event or payment) for over 12 months. However, we will attempt to warn you by email before terminating your account to provide you with an opportunity to log in to your account so that it remains active.

7.1. Legal Status. If you are an individual, you may only use the Service if you have the power to form a contract with SurveyMonkey. None of the Services are intended for use by individuals less than 13 years old. If you are under 13 years old or do not have the power to form a contract with SurveyMonkey, you may not use the Services. We recommend that parents and guardians directly supervise any use of the Services by minors. If you are not an individual, you warrant that you are validly formed and existing under the laws of your jurisdiction of formation and that you have duly authorized your agent to bind you to these Terms.

7.2. Embargoes. You may only use the Services if you are not barred under any applicable laws from doing so. If you are located in a country embargoed by United States or other applicable law from receiving the Services, or are on the U.S. Department of Commerce's Denied Persons List or Entity List, or the U.S. Treasury Department's list of Specially Designated Nationals, you are not permitted to purchase any paid Services from SurveyMonkey.

8.1. Legal Compliance. You must use the Services in compliance with, and only as permitted by, applicable law.

8.2. Your Responsibilities. You are responsible for your conduct, Content, and communications with others while using the Services. You must comply with the following requirements when using the Services:

(a) You may not misuse our Services by interfering with their normal operation, or attempting to access them using a method other than through the interfaces and instructions that we provide.

(b) You may not circumvent or attempt to circumvent any limitations that SurveyMonkey imposes on your account (such as by opening up a new account to conduct a survey that we have closed for a Terms violation).

(c) Unless authorized by SurveyMonkey in writing, you may not probe, scan, or test the vulnerability of any SurveyMonkey system or network.

(d) Unless permitted by applicable law, you may not deny others access to, or reverse engineer, the Services, or attempt to do so.

(e) You may not transmit any viruses, malware, or other types of malicious software, or links to such software, through the Services.

(f) You may not engage in abusive or excessive usage of the Services, which is usage significantly in excess of average usage patterns that adversely affects the speed, responsiveness, stability, availability, or functionality of the Services for other users. SurveyMonkey will endeavor to notify you of any abusive or excessive usage to provide you with an opportunity to reduce such usage to a level acceptable to SurveyMonkey.

(g) You may not use the Services to infringe the intellectual property rights of others, or to commit an unlawful activity.

(h) Unless authorized by SurveyMonkey in writing, you may not resell or lease the Services.

(i) If your use of the Services requires you to comply with industry-specific regulations applicable to such use, you will be solely responsible for such compliance, unless SurveyMonkey has agreed with you otherwise. You may not use the Services in a way that would subject SurveyMonkey to those industry-specific regulations without obtaining SurveyMonkey's prior written agreement. For example, you may not use the Services to collect, protect, or otherwise handle "protected health information" (as defined in 45 C.F.R. §160.103 under United States federal regulations) without entering into a separate business associate agreement with SurveyMonkey that permits you to do so.

9.1. By You. If you terminate a Subscription in the middle of a billing cycle, you will not receive a refund for any period of time you did not use in that billing cycle unless you are terminating the Agreement for our breach and have so notified us in writing, or unless a refund is required by law.

9.2. By SurveyMonkey. SurveyMonkey may limit, suspend, or stop providing the Services to you if you fail to comply with these Terms (such as a failure to pay fees when due), or if you use the Services in a way that causes legal liability to us or disrupts others' use of the Services. SurveyMonkey may also suspend providing the Services to you if we are investigating suspected misconduct by you. If we suspend or terminate the Services you receive, we will endeavor to give you advance notice and an opportunity to export a copy of your Content from that Service. However, there may be time sensitive situations where SurveyMonkey may decide that we need to take immediate action without notice. SurveyMonkey has no obligation to retain your Content upon termination of the applicable Service.

9.3. Further Measures. If SurveyMonkey stops providing the Services to you because you repeatedly or egregiously breach these Terms, SurveyMonkey may take measures to prevent the further use of the Services by you, including blocking your IP address.

10.1. Changes to Terms. SurveyMonkey may change these Terms at any time for a variety of reasons, such as to reflect changes in applicable law or updates to Services, and to account for new Services or functionality. Any changes will be posted to the location at which those terms appear. SurveyMonkey may also provide notification of changes on its blog or via email. Changes will be effective no sooner than the day they are publicly posted. In order for certain changes to become effective, applicable law may require SurveyMonkey to obtain your consent to such changes, or to provide you with sufficient advance notice of them. If you do not want to agree to any changes made to the terms for a Service, you should stop using that Service, because by continuing to use the Services you indicate your agreement to be bound by the updated terms.

10.2. Changes to Services. SurveyMonkey constantly changes and improves the Services. SurveyMonkey may add, alter, or remove functionality from a Service at any time without prior notice. SurveyMonkey may also limit, suspend, or discontinue a Service at its discretion. If SurveyMonkey discontinues a Service, we will give you reasonable advance notice to provide you with an opportunity to export a copy of your Content from that Service. SurveyMonkey may remove content from the Services at any time in our sole discretion, although we will endeavor to notify you before we do that if it materially impacts you and if practicable under the circumstances.

11.1. Disclaimers. While it is in SurveyMonkey's interest to provide you with a great experience when using the Services (and we love to please our customers), there are certain things we do not promise about them. We try to keep our online Services up, but they may be unavailable from time to time for various reasons. EXCEPT AS EXPRESSLY PROVIDED IN THESE TERMS AND TO THE EXTENT PERMITTED BY APPLICABLE LAW, THE SERVICES ARE PROVIDED "AS IS" AND SURVEYMONKEY DOES NOT MAKE WARRANTIES OF ANY KIND, EXPRESS, IMPLIED, OR STATUTORY, INCLUDING THOSE OF MERCHANTABILITY, FITNESS FOR A PARTICULAR PURPOSE, AND NON-INFRINGEMENT OR ANY REGARDING AVAILABILITY, RELIABILITY, OR ACCURACY OF THE SERVICES.

11.2. Exclusion of Certain Liability. TO THE EXTENT PERMITTED BY APPLICABLE LAW, SURVEYMONKEY, ITS AFFILIATES, OFFICERS, EMPLOYEES, AGENTS, SUPPLIERS, AND LICENSORS WILL NOT BE LIABLE FOR ANY INDIRECT, CONSEQUENTIAL, SPECIAL, INCIDENTAL, PUNITIVE, OR EXEMPLARY DAMAGES WHATSOEVER, INCLUDING DAMAGES FOR LOST PROFITS, LOSS OF USE, LOSS OF DATA, ARISING OUT OF OR IN CONNECTION WITH THE SERVICES AND THESE TERMS, AND WHETHER BASED ON CONTRACT, TORT, STRICT LIABILITY, OR ANY OTHER LEGAL THEORY, EVEN IF SURVEYMONKEY HAS BEEN ADVISED OF THE

POSSIBILITY OF SUCH DAMAGES AND EVEN IF A REMEDY FAILS OF ITS ESSENTIAL PURPOSE.

11.3. Limitation of Liability. TO THE EXTENT PERMITTED BY APPLICABLE LAW, THE AGGREGATE LIABILITY OF EACH OF SURVEYMONKEY, ITS AFFILIATES, OFFICERS, EMPLOYEES, AGENTS, SUPPLIERS, AND LICENSORS ARISING OUT OF OR IN CONNECTION WITH THE SERVICES AND THESE TERMS WILL NOT EXCEED THE GREATER OF: (A) THE AMOUNTS PAID BY YOU TO SURVEYMONKEY FOR USE OF THE SERVICES AT ISSUE DURING THE 3 MONTHS PRIOR TO THE EVENT GIVING RISE TO THE LIABILITY; AND (B) US$25.00.

11.4. Consumers. We acknowledge that the laws of certain jurisdictions provide legal rights to consumers that may not be overridden by contract or waived by those consumers. If you are such a consumer, nothing in these Terms limits any of those consumer rights.

11.5. Businesses. If you are a business, you will indemnify and hold harmless SurveyMonkey and its affiliates, officers, agents, and employees from all liabilities, damages, and costs (including settlement costs and reasonable attorneys' fees) arising out of a third-party claim regarding or in connection with your use of the Services or a breach of these Terms, to the extent that such liabilities, damages and costs were caused by you.

12.1. Who you are contracting with? Unless otherwise specified in relation to a particular Service, the Services are provided by, and you are contracting with, SurveyMonkey Inc.

12.2. SurveyMonkey Inc. For any Service provided by SurveyMonkey Inc., the following provisions will apply to any terms governing that Service:

- **Contracting Entity.** References to "**SurveyMonkey**", "**we**", "**us**", and "**our**" are references to SurveyMonkey Inc., located at 101 Lytton Avenue, Palo Alto, CA 94301, United States of America.

- **Governing Law.** Those terms are governed by the laws of the State of California (without regard to its conflict of law's provisions).

- **Jurisdiction.** Except if prohibited by applicable law, each party submits to the exclusive jurisdiction of the state courts located in Santa Clara County, California, and the federal courts located in the Northern District of California with respect to the subject matter of those terms.

12.3. SurveyMonkey Europe Sarl. For any Service provided by SurveyMonkey Europe Sarl, the following provisions will apply to any terms governing that Service:

- **Contracting Entity.** References to "**SurveyMonkey**", "**we**", "**us**", and "**our**" are references to SurveyMonkey Europe Sarl, located at 1, Allée Scheffer, L-2520 Luxembourg.

- **Governing Law.** Those terms are governed by the laws of Luxembourg (without regard to its conflicts of law's provisions).

- **Jurisdiction.** Except if prohibited by applicable law, in relation to any legal action or proceedings to enforce those terms or arising out of or in connection with those terms, each party irrevocably submits to the exclusive jurisdiction of the courts of the city of Luxembourg, Grand Duchy of Luxembourg.

Assignment. You may not assign these Terms without SurveyMonkey's prior written consent, which may be withheld in SurveyMonkey's sole discretion. SurveyMonkey may assign these Terms at any time without notice to you.

Entire Agreement. These Terms (including the Additional Terms) constitute the entire agreement between you and SurveyMonkey, and they supersede any other prior or contemporaneous agreements, terms and conditions, written or oral concerning its subject matter. Any terms and conditions appearing on a purchase order or similar document issued by you do not apply to the Services, do not override or form a part of these Terms, and are void.

Independent Contractors. The relationship between you and SurveyMonkey is that of independent contractors, and not legal partners, employees, or agents of each other.

Interpretation. The use of the terms "includes", "including", "such as", and similar terms, will be deemed not to limit what else might be included.

No Waiver. A party's failure or delay to enforce a provision under these Terms is not a waiver of its right to do so later.

Precedence. To the extent any conflict exists, the Additional Terms prevail over this TOU with respect to the Services to which the Additional Terms apply.

Severability. If any provision of these Terms is determined to be unenforceable by a court of competent jurisdiction, that provision will be severed and the remainder of terms will remain in full effect.

Third Party Beneficiaries. There are no third-party beneficiaries to these Terms.

Source:
SurveyMonkey, http://www.surveymonkey.com/mp/policy/terms-of-use